FOUNDATIONS FOR KIDS

A 260-DAY BIBLE READING PLAN FOR KIDS

Robby & Kandi Gallaty
LifeWay Press®
Nashville, TN

ISBN 978-1-430063-31-5
Item 005790788

Dewey Decimal Classification Number: 268.432
Subject Heading: Discipleship—Curricula\God\Bible—Study
Dewey Decimal Classification Number: 248.82
Subject Heading: CHRISTIAN LIFE \ JESUS CHRIST--TEACHINGS

We believe that the Bible has God for its author; salvation for its end; and truth, without
any mixture of error, for its matter and that all Scripture is totally true and trustworthy.
To review LifeWay's doctrinal guideline, please visit www.lifeway.com/doctrinalguideline.

Printed in the United States of America

Replicate Ministries and LifeWay Kids
LifeWay Resources
One LifeWay Plaza
Nashville, TN 37234-0172

ABOUT THE AUTHORS

ROBBY GALLATY is the senior pastor of Long Hollow Baptist Church in Hendersonville, Tennessee. He was radically saved from a life of drug and alcohol addiction. In 2008 he founded Replicate Ministries to educate, equip, and empower people to be disciples who make disciple-makers (replicate.org). He's the author of *The Forgotten Jesus: How Western Christians Should Follow an Eastern Rabbi* (2017), *Rediscovering Discipleship: Making Jesus' Final Words Our First Work* (2015), and *Here and Now: Thriving in the Kingdom of Heaven Today* (2019).

KANDI GALLATY has been investing in the lives of women for over a decade. She believes that there are three major sources to draw from when investing in the lives of others: God's Word, God's work in one's life, and God's Spirit. She is passionate about cultivating a biblical worldview from the truths of Scripture and teaching women how to steward the life experiences and lessons God has allowed in their lives. Kandi and her husband, Robby, live in Nashville, TN, and are the proud parents of two boys Rig (8) and Ryder (6).

MELISSA SWAIN is a wife, mom, teacher, and writer. Melissa has written and edited books, blogs, and journals for various authors and pastors as well as LifeWay Christian Resources. Melissa and her husband, Chris, have lived all over the south serving in various aspects of ministry, but now call Nashville, Tennessee, home along with their two children and Boston Terrier.

ROBBY GALLATY ON THE HEAR METHOD

My wife, Kandi, and I developed, along with the help of our Replicate team, a reading plan called Foundations 260. The F-260 is a 260-day reading plan that highlights the foundational passages of Scripture every disciple should know. After failed attempts of reading through the Bible in a year with previous discipleship groups, I wanted a manageable plan that believers who had never read the Bible before could complete. In order to digest more of the Word, the F-260 encourages believers to read less and to keep a H.E.A.R. journal.

The acronym H.E.A.R. stands for Highlight, Explain, Apply, and Respond. Each of these four steps contributes to creating an atmosphere to hear God speak. After settling on a reading plan and establishing a time for studying God's Word, you will be ready to H.E.A.R. from God.

Notice that all of the words in the H.E.A.R. formula are action words: Highlight, Explain, Apply, and Respond. God does not want us to sit back and wait for Him to drop some truth into our laps. Instead of waiting passively, God desires that we actively pursue Him.

MEMORIZING SCRIPTURE
While many plans for memorizing Scripture are effective, a simple system has been effective for me. All you need is a pack of index cards and a committed desire to memorize God's Word. It's easy: write the reference of the verse on one side of the card and the text of the verse on the other. Focus on five verses at a time, and carry your pack of Scripture cards with you.

Throughout the day, whenever you have a few minutes, pull out your pack of Scripture cards and review them. Read the reference first, followed by the verse. Continue to recite the verse until you get a feel for the flow of the passage. When you are comfortable with the text, look only at the reference side of the card in order to test your recall.

NOW ... FOUNDATIONS FOR KIDS!
We believe that discipleship starts at home. It was always a dream that as parents went through *Foundations*, they could lead their kids through a similar resource. Now you have it—*Foundations for Kids*! Together you will go through the HEAR method this way:

HIGHLIGHT Each day, has a passage for younger kids to read and a passage for older kids to read, plus the memory verse for the week. Each day kids will have the opportunity to read and memorize Scripture.

EXPLAIN Each day, will have four bullets: three bullets are shorter and can be read by all kids. The fourth bullet will be longer for older kids. The fourth bullet may give additional information from extra verses or be written to an older kids level.

APPLY Every day, kids will have a learning activity to help them apply the Bible truth through a game, question, or puzzle.

RESPOND Kids will have the opportunity to respond in prayer.

PARENTS

Parents, help your kids go through the HEAR method each day. Younger Kids may need you to read for them and lead them through each day's devotion. Beginning readers will grow stronger each day and may only need occasional help. Middle and older kids will be able to read on their own each day. Regardless of your child's age, spend time discussing the day's reading and how he or she can apply God's truth to everyday life.

BEST TIPS

WHEN: Set a regular time for your time together with God.

WHERE: Find a comfortable, quiet place where you won't be disturbed.

WHY: Communicate with your kids that God wants to have a relationship with them. God speaks through the Bible, when you pray, and through fellowship with others—all ways your kids can hear God speak as you go through *Foundations for Kids*.

WHAT: Gather your Bible, *Foundations for Kids*, and a pencil or markers.

HOW: Explain how important the Bible is. Teach Bible skills as you go. Follow these steps:

1. Pray and ask God to be with your time together and to speak to you. Pray that you will listen and learn.
2. Read the passage from the Bible.
3. Ask your kids what they think the passage means. Read together through Explain and talk about the passage and what it means.
4. Complete the Application activity together.
5. Review the memory verse for the week. Create a verse card to review and practice learning.
6. Pray together.
7. Hug your kids, tell them how much you love them, and tell them how thankful you are that you could spend this time together with God.

WEEK 1
DAY 1

HIGHLIGHT

OLDER KIDS: Genesis 1:27-2:2
YOUNGER KIDS: Genesis 1:31-2:2
MEMORY VERSE: Genesis 1:27

EXPLAIN

- God created the entire universe and everything in it.
- God made us in His own image.
- God gave us instructions to be in charge of the earth and to care for it.
- God designed all things to do unique jobs on earth, and by doing their jobs they bring Him glory. People were created to have a relationship with God.

APPLY

In just six days, God created everything! And not only did God create everything, God said everything He made was very good. God didn't say, "Oops! I don't think I like that animal, maybe I'll try again." He made everything perfectly to bring Him glory. Draw a picture of something from God's creation.

RESPOND

PRAY: Jesus, thank You for creating everything. I want to bring You glory in everything I do.

HIGHLIGHT

OLDER KIDS: Genesis 3:8-13
YOUNGER KIDS: Genesis 3:8-10
MEMORY VERSE: Genesis 1:27

EXPLAIN

- Adam and Eve chose to break God's law. Our actions when we break God's law are called sins.
- Because Adam and Eve chose to sin, we are all sinners.
- Sin separates us from God because He is holy. God sent His Son Jesus to rescue us from sin.
- Adam and Eve were the first people God created, and they were also the first ones to sin. Because they brought sin into the world, everyone is born with sin. God sent Jesus to live a sinless life so that He could rescue us from sin.

APPLY

After Adam and Eve sinned, they were afraid and hid from God in the garden. But we can't hide from God because He knows everything! Trace each snake and match its number and letter to those in the box to complete each statement.

RESPOND

PRAY: Heavenly Father, thank You for sending Jesus to rescue us from sin.

USE THE SNAKE MAZE IF YOU NEED HELP!

(1) Adam and Eve...

(2) Breaking God's law is called...

(3) God Sent Jesus...

(4) Because God is Holy,

(5) Sin is something...

(6) Adam and eve hid from...

(7) The first people to sin were...

(8) Because Adam and Eve sinned...

(A) to rescue us from sin.

(B) everyone is born with.

(C) sin separates us from Him.

(D) sin

(E) broke God's law

(F) we Are Sinners.

(G) Adam and Eve.

(H) God.

HIGHLIGHT

OLDER KIDS: Genesis 7:1-6
YOUNGER KIDS: Genesis 7:1-5
MEMORY VERSE: Genesis 1:27

EXPLAIN

- The world became so full of sin that God wanted to destroy it. Because Noah followed God, God did not punish Noah and his family.
- God is serious about sin and will not let it go unpunished.
- God gave Noah instructions to build the ark that saved his family and the animals from the flood.
- The world was so sinful, it made God very sad. Noah was the only person who followed God. God decided to destroy all life on the earth except for Noah's family and the animals that He would send to the ark.

APPLY

Because Noah followed God, God gave Noah's family a rescue plan—the ark. Noah obeyed God, and his family was saved from the flood. God's ultimate rescue plan for us was His Son Jesus, who lived a sinless life but took the punishment for our sin anyway. Complete the dot-to-dot picture of the ark and draw your favorite animal or animals inside.

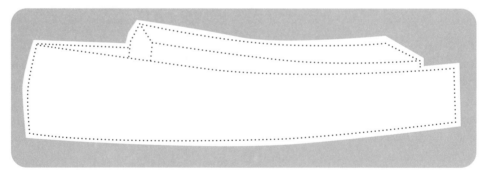

RESPOND

PRAY: God, thank You for loving us and forgiving us of our sin.

HIGHLIGHT

OLDER KIDS: Genesis 9:12-17
YOUNGER KIDS: Genesis 9:13-15
MEMORY VERSE: Genesis 1:27

EXPLAIN

- God made a promise to Noah that He would never flood the entire earth again.
- God made a rainbow as a reminder of His promise.
- God always keeps His promises.
- God made a promise never to destroy the earth with a flood again. To confirm His promise, God presented a rainbow.

APPLY

Has someone ever broken a promise they made you? Every time we see a rainbow, we can remember God's promise and how God always keeps His promises. As you color the rainbow, think about some of God's promises to us.

COLOR THE RAINBOW USING THESE COLORS IN ORDER.

RESPOND

PRAY: God, thank You for always keeping Your promises. Thank You also for rainbows, which are reminders of Your promise to Noah.

WEEK 1
DAY 5

OLDER KIDS: Job 1:6-12,22
YOUNGER KIDS: Job 1:8-12,22
MEMORY VERSE: Genesis 1:27

 EXPLAIN

- Satan thought Job followed God only because God protected Job from suffering.
- God allowed Satan to destroy Job's belongings and harm his family.
- Sometimes God allows suffering, even when it is not caused by sin.
- Satan thought if he made Job suffer, Job would sin or blame God. But Job didn't sin or blame God for his suffering.

 APPLY

Has someone ever been mean to you for no reason? We do not always understand why bad things happen, but bad things are not always the consequences of sin. Talk with a parent about why we should obey God all the time. Discuss the following questions:

- Why do we obey God?
- What does the story of Job teach us?
- Is it easier or harder to obey God when things are going well?
- Is it easier or harder to obey God when things are going poorly?
- How can we choose to love and obey God no matter how we feel?

 **RESPOND**

PRAY: Heavenly Father, help me not to sin when I go through times of suffering.

 HIGHLIGHT

OLDER KIDS: Job 38:1-7
YOUNGER KIDS: Job 38:1-4
MEMORY VERSE: Hebrews 11:8

 EXPLAIN

- Job was feeling sorry for himself and asked God why he was suffering. God answered him.
- God reminded Job that He is the One who created the earth.
- God continues this chapter by reminding Job that He created everything and knows everything.
- Have you ever been surprised? God can't be surprised! Nothing happens that God doesn't know about. Because God created everything, He is in control of everything!

 APPLY

Sometimes we need to be reminded that even when we don't understand what is going on, God is in control of everything. Write down or draw a picture of a time you were surprised or didn't understand what was going on. Did God know what was happening? (Yes!)

 RESPOND

PRAY: God, thank You for being in control of everything. Help me remember You are in control even when I'm surprised or don't understand.

OLDER KIDS: Job 42:1-6,10
YOUNGER KIDS: Job 42:1-3,10
MEMORY VERSE: Hebrews 11:8

EXPLAIN

- Job remembered God can do anything, and nothing can get in the way of His plans.
- Job saw for himself God's grace and repented from his bad attitude toward suffering.
- God restored Job and blessed him with more than he had before.
- Have you ever felt like you were suffering and no one understood? Job felt that way, too. But after God finished talking, Job remembered God could do anything, and nothing can get in the way of His plans. Job understood God had been in control the whole time!

APPLY

After Job repented, God gave Job twice as many things as he had before and restored his family. Solve the puzzle to discover what Job remembered.

RESPOND

PRAY: God, thank You for being in control even when we suffer! Help me to remember that You are in charge and nothing can get in the way of Your plans.

HIGHLIGHT

OLDER KIDS: Genesis 12:1-5a
YOUNGER KIDS: Genesis 12:1-3
MEMORY VERSE: Hebrews 11:8

EXPLAIN

- God told Abram to take his family, leave his home, and go to a new place.
- God made a promise to Abram: if Abram followed God, then He would make Abram's name great and bless all the people of the world through him.
- Abram had faith in God, so he followed God's instructions.
- Have your parents ever taken you on a surprise trip or vacation? You didn't know where you were going until you got there, but your parents knew the whole time. Abram's trip was like that— God knew where Abram was going, even though he didn't. Abram had faith that God knew the destination.

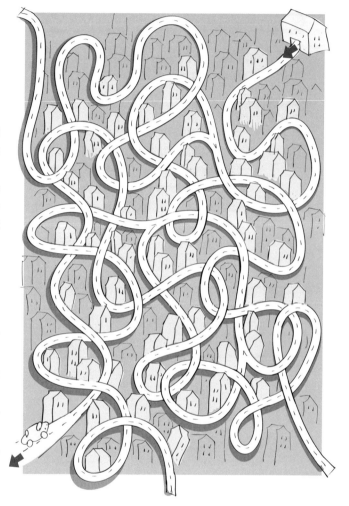

APPLY

Abram followed God, even when he wasn't sure where he would end up. Imagine what it might feel like to leave home without being sure of where you would end up. Work through the maze to see how Abram might have felt as he followed God's instructions to leave his home.

RESPOND

PRAY: God, thank You for giving me instructions on how to follow You. Help me have faith as I follow Your instructions.

HIGHLIGHT

OLDER KIDS: Genesis 15:2-6
YOUNGER KIDS: Genesis 15:4-6
MEMORY VERSE: Hebrews 11:8

EXPLAIN

- God promised that Abram's family would grow into a great nation, but Abram didn't understand how this could happen because he didn't have any kids.
- God showed Abram the stars in the sky and said that he would have as many offspring as there were stars.
- Abram believed God and had faith, or trusted, He would do what He said.
- God showed Abram the stars and said that he would have as many offspring as the stars in the sky. Because Abram had faith in God, he believed Him, even though he and his wife Sarai were old and didn't have kids yet.

APPLY

Have you ever tried to count the stars? There are too many for us to count! Even though we can't count the stars, God can. Draw what you think the sky might have looked like the night God showed Abram the stars.

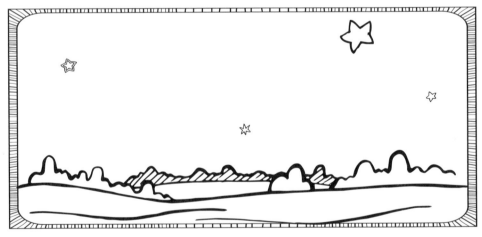

RESPOND

PRAY: Heavenly Father, thank You for knowing the number of stars there are in the sky. Help me to have faith like Abram did, even when I don't understand Your plan.

 **HIGHLIGHT**

OLDER KIDS: Genesis 17:1-8
YOUNGER KIDS: Genesis 17:3-8
MEMORY VERSE: Hebrews 11:8

 EXPLAIN

- God made a covenant (special promise) with Abram to make him the father of many nations.
- As part of His covenant, God changed Abram's name to Abraham.
- God's covenant was not just for Abraham, but for his future children, too.
- A *covenant* is a promise between two people or between a person and God. Through Jesus, God made a covenant to rescue us from sin. We can trust in God to keep His promises.

APPLY

As part of God's covenant, He changed Abram's name to Abraham, which means "the father of a multitude." Abraham's new name was a reminder of God's covenant. If you were to change your name as a reminder of God's promises, which promise would you want to remember?

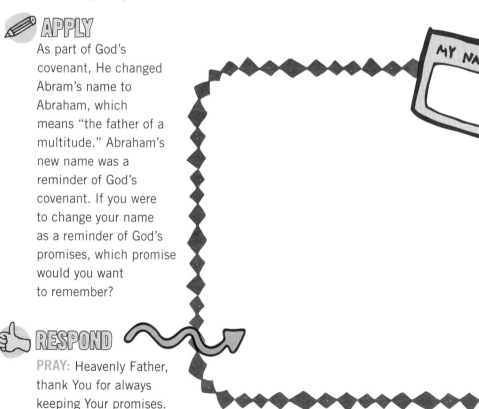

MY NAME IS

RESPOND

PRAY: Heavenly Father, thank You for always keeping Your promises.

 HIGHLIGHT

OLDER KIDS: Genesis 18:9-15
YOUNGER KIDS: Genesis 18:13-14
MEMORY VERSE: Romans 4:20

EXPLAIN

- The Lord visited Abraham and Sarah at the tent where they lived.
- The Lord said He would visit them again in one year and by that time, Sarah would have a baby.
- Sarah wondered if she was too old to have a baby, even though God had already promised she would.
- God had made a promise to multiply Abraham's family, even when he and Sarah didn't have any kids. When Sarah heard the Lord say she would have a baby boy, she laughed because she was old. But the Lord reminded Abraham and Sarah that nothing is impossible or too hard for God.

 APPLY

God created everything, knows everything, and is in charge of everything. Look at the pictures and write the first letter of each word in the blank above to discover what is impossible for God.

RESPOND

PRAY: Heavenly Father, help me remember that nothing is impossible for You.

HIGHLIGHT

OLDER KIDS: Genesis 21:1-5
YOUNGER KIDS: Genesis 21:1-3
MEMORY VERSE: Romans 4:20

EXPLAIN

- Just as God promised, Sarah gave birth to a baby boy.
- Abraham named their son Isaac.
- The name *Isaac* means "he laughs."
- God kept His promise and gave Abraham and Sarah a son. They named him Isaac. Abraham and Sarah were very old when Isaac was born and did not think it was possible to have a baby so late in life. But we know God keeps His promises and nothing is too hard for Him!

APPLY

Yesterday, we learned that Sarah laughed when God said she would have a baby. Today, we hear how God fulfilled His promise! God is always faithful to keep His promises, even when we forget or lack faith. God's promises do not change, even when we sin. Which elephant's trunk is reaching toward a *true* statement?

RESPOND

PRAY: God, thank You for always keeping Your promises.

ABRAHAM LAUGHED.

THE BABY WAS A GIRL.

GOD KEPT HIS PROMISE.

 **HIGHLIGHT**

OLDER KIDS: Genesis 22:1-2,9-12
YOUNGER KIDS: Genesis 22:9-12
MEMORY VERSE: Romans 4:20

 EXPLAIN

- God tested Abraham by asking him to sacrifice (give as an offering) his son Isaac.
- Isaac showed he was willing to do what his father said.
- God stopped Abraham before Isaac was hurt. God gave Abraham a ram to sacrifice instead of Isaac.
- Abraham must have had a hard time understanding why God would ask him to sacrifice his son, Isaac. Ultimately, God provided a ram for Abraham to sacrifice, and Isaac was rescued.

 APPLY

God sent Jesus to be the perfect sacrifice for our sin. Because of Jesus, we are rescued from sin just like Isaac was rescued because of the ram. Color the picture of the ram.

 RESPOND

PRAY: Heavenly Father, thank You for sending Jesus so we can be rescued from sin.

 **HIGHLIGHT**

OLDER KIDS: Genesis 24:12-15
YOUNGER KIDS: Genesis 24:14-15
MEMORY VERSE: Romans 4:20

 EXPLAIN

- Abraham sent a servant to find a wife for Isaac.
- The servant prayed for God to show him the woman that would be Isaac's wife.
- Rebekah was the woman God chose to be Isaac's wife.
- Abraham sent a servant back to his homeland to find a wife for Isaac. The servant had to trust God to show him the woman He had chosen for Isaac. He prayed that God would show her to him through her kindness. Rebekah was the woman God had chosen to become Isaac's wife.

 APPLY

Part of God's promise to make Abraham a great nation was that Isaac must have a wife. God had already planned for Rebekah to become Isaac's wife. God is always working to fulfill His promises. Circle the shadow that perfectly matches Rebekah.

 **RESPOND**

PRAY: God, thank You for always working to fulfill Your promises.

OLDER KIDS: Genesis 25:27-34
YOUNGER KIDS: Genesis 25:29-34
MEMORY VERSE: Romans 4:20

 EXPLAIN

- Isaac and Rebekah had twin sons, Esau and Jacob.
- Esau and Jacob were members of Abraham's family, so they were part of God's promise that Abraham would become a great nation.
- Esau sold his birthright to Jacob, which meant that the blessings (special gifts) meant for Esau went to Jacob.
- Esau and Jacob fought with each other from birth. Jacob wanted Esau's birthright (a special blessing from their father) and found a way to get Esau to sell it to him.

 APPLY

Jacob wanted something that didn't belong to him and sneakily found a way to get it. Jesus freely shared his birthright and special blessings with us when He paid the price for our sins on the cross. With a parent, discuss why a gift freely given to you is better than something you got by being sneaky.

 **RESPOND**

PRAY: Jesus, thank You for sharing Your birthright and blessings with us by paying the price for our sin on the cross.

HIGHLIGHT

OLDER KIDS: Genesis 28:10-15
YOUNGER KIDS: Genesis 28:13-15
MEMORY VERSE: 1 John 3:18

EXPLAIN

- Jacob ran away because Esau was angry. Jacob had tricked his father, Isaac, into giving him the family blessing instead of Esau.
- God's promise to Abraham and Isaac was for Jacob as well, and God reminded Jacob of this promise in a dream.
- Even after Jacob sinned, God was still working toward keeping His promise.
- Jacob had been sneaky in getting Esau to sell his birthright, and then he tricked their father Isaac into giving him the family blessing instead of Esau. Esau was angry and wanted to kill Jacob. Even while the two brothers were fighting, God was working to keep His promise to Esau and Jacob.

APPLY

Even though Jacob sinned and had to run away, God's promise did not change. God did not leave Jacob. He reminded him that his offspring would be as plentiful as the dust of the earth and all people would be blessed through him. Use the table on the right to decode the second half of this message.

GOD IS ALWAYS WORKING TO FULFILL HIS PROMISES.

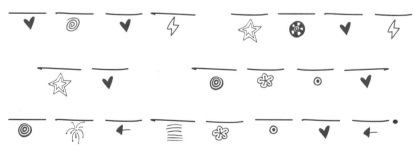

RESPOND

PRAY: Heavenly Father, thank You for always working to fulfill Your promises, even when we make mistakes.

A	✿
B	☾
C	●
D	♣
E	♥
F	★
G	✚
H	✹
I	✺
J	✎
K	⊙
L	☺
M	◎
N	ϟ
O	⠿
P	☆
Q	☀
R	→
S	←
T	≡
U	∿
V	◎
W	☆
X	●
Y	✹
Z	●

 **HIGHLIGHT**

OLDER KIDS: Genesis 29:21-28
YOUNGER KIDS: Genesis 29:21-25
MEMORY VERSE: 1 John 3:18

 EXPLAIN

- Jacob loved Rachel and wanted to marry her, but Laban tricked him into marrying Leah instead.
- Jacob agreed to work for Laban seven more years so he could marry Rachel.
- Jacob had tricked his own brother and father, and then he himself was tricked.
- Jacob had been a deceiver among his own family. Now Laban tricked Jacob. God was still working on Jacob's heart to bring Jacob back to Him.

 APPLY

While Jacob and Laban were tricking people, God was still working on His promise. God can use us even after we sin because He has the power to change our hearts and our attitudes. Discuss: What is something God can help you change your attitude about?

 RESPOND

PRAY: God, thank You for having the power to change my heart and attitude.

 ## HIGHLIGHT

OLDER KIDS: Genesis 32:24-30
YOUNGER KIDS: Genesis 32:24-28
MEMORY VERSE: 1 John 3:18

EXPLAIN

- For the first time since he ran away, Jacob was on his way to meet Esau.
- God came and wrestled with Jacob all night long. Jacob wouldn't let go until the man blessed him.
- God blessed Jacob and gave him a new name, *Israel*.
- Jacob was taking his family to meet Esau, and during the night, God came to wrestle with him. Jacob was unwilling to let the man go unless He blessed him. The blessing that the man gave to Jacob was a new name—*Israel*. *Israel* became the name of God's chosen people.

 ## APPLY

God changed Jacob's name, which became the name of the entire nation of God's people. When we become part of God's family, we receive a new name, too. We are called the children of God. To discover Jacob's new name, begin with the "I" in the center and follow the directions below, writing each new letter in the box.

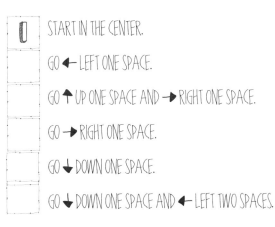

I — START IN THE CENTER.

GO ← LEFT ONE SPACE.

GO ↑ UP ONE SPACE AND → RIGHT ONE SPACE.

GO → RIGHT ONE SPACE.

GO ↓ DOWN ONE SPACE.

GO ↓ DOWN ONE SPACE AND ← LEFT TWO SPACES.

 ## RESPOND

PRAY: God, thank You for allowing us to become part of Your family.

HIGHLIGHT

OLDER KIDS: Genesis 33:4-9
YOUNGER KIDS: Genesis 33:4-5
MEMORY VERSE: 1 John 3:18

EXPLAIN

- Jacob and his family had traveled to meet Esau. Jacob was worried his brother would still be angry.
- Esau wasn't angry anymore. He gave Jacob a big hug!
- Jacob gave Esau gifts, but Esau wasn't interested in them. He was happy Jacob was home and had brought his family.
- Jacob was nervous to see Esau again because he wasn't sure Esau had forgiven him. He even took gifts to give Esau in case he was still angry. But Esau wasn't angry, he was happy to see Jacob and his family.

APPLY

Sometimes when we're angry, it is hard to forgive. Esau forgave Jacob for tricking him and their father. God forgives us of our sin because Jesus paid the price for us. We forgive others because God forgives us. Work through the maze to help Jacob find Esau.

RESPOND

PRAY: Jesus, thank You for paying the price for our sin so we can be forgiven and forgive others.

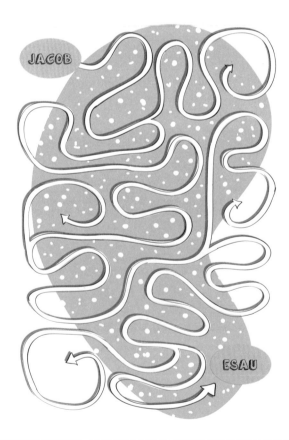

HIGHLIGHT

OLDER KIDS: Genesis 37:23-28
YOUNGER KIDS: Genesis 37:23-24,28
MEMORY VERSE: 1 John 3:18

EXPLAIN

- Joseph was Jacob's favorite son, and Jacob gave Joseph a colorful robe. Joseph's brothers hated him because he was their father's favorite.
- Joseph's brothers decided to get rid of him, but they didn't want to hurt him.
- Joseph's brothers sold him as a slave to traders who were on their way to Egypt.
- Joseph was his father's favorite son, which made his older brothers angry. They didn't like that he was given special treatment. So one day, when Joseph went to them out in the field, they took away his special robe and eventually sold him. They never wanted to see him again.

APPLY

Joseph was treated unfairly by his brothers. He had to suffer through some hard times because of other people's actions. But God was still working! What the brothers meant for harm, God would use to bring good later. Draw and color a picture of Joseph wearing his colorful robe.

RESPOND

PRAY: God, thank You for working even when I go through hard times.

HIGHLIGHT

OLDER KIDS: Genesis 39:21-23
YOUNGER KIDS: Genesis 39:22
MEMORY VERSE: Romans 8:28

EXPLAIN

- Joseph was sold as a slave to Potiphar. Then Potiphar's wife told a lie about Joseph, and he was put in prison.
- God didn't leave Joseph when he went to prison!
- The warden put Joseph in charge of all the prisoners.
- Joseph had been a slave in Potiphar's house for a while, and he had served his master well. Joseph also followed God. Potiphar's wife told a lie about Joseph, and Joseph was sent to prison. God did not leave Joseph just because he was in prison. Joseph was faithful to God, and God blessed Joseph even in prison. The warden put Joseph in charge of all the prisoners.

APPLY

Sometimes things happen that we don't understand. God doesn't leave us when these things happen. Starting with the word *WENT*, follow the instructions from arrow to arrow. Place each word in its corresponding blank.

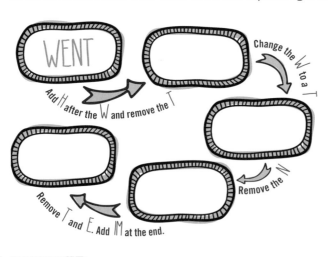

Joseph __WENT__ to

prison _____

his master's wife

lied about him.

_____,

Joseph was faithful,

and God was with

him. _____ warden

put _____

in charge of all the

prisoners.

RESPOND

PRAY: Heavenly Father, thank You for always being with me.

HIGHLIGHT

OLDER KIDS: Genesis 41:38-42
YOUNGER KIDS: Genesis 41:39-41
MEMORY VERSE: Romans 8:28

EXPLAIN

- God gave Joseph the power to tell two of Pharaoh's workers what their dreams meant while they were in prison together.
- When Pharaoh had bad dreams, one of the workers remembered Joseph, so Pharaoh called Joseph to the palace to tell him what his dreams meant.
- God gave Joseph the power to tell Pharaoh what his dreams meant. Pharaoh saw how wise God had made Joseph, and he put Joseph in charge of the entire nation of Egypt.
- Joseph continued to follow God while he was in prison. He told some of Pharaoh's workers what their dreams meant. After the workers went back to the palace, Pharaoh had bad dreams. One of the workers remembered Joseph. God gave Joseph the power to tell Pharaoh what his dreams meant. Pharaoh saw how wise Joseph was and put him in charge of the entire nation of Egypt.

APPLY

Joseph went from being in prison to being in charge of Egypt! God had a plan for Joseph and was working to carry out His plan, even when Joseph didn't understand the things that were happening. Look up Romans 8:28 and write it here.

RESPOND

PRAY: God, thank You for always working, even when things happen that I don't understand.

HIGHLIGHT

OLDER KIDS: Genesis 42:5-8
YOUNGER KIDS: Genesis 42:5-6
MEMORY VERSE: Romans 8:28

EXPLAIN

- The dreams Joseph interpreted for Pharaoh foretold a famine, and Joseph prepared by storing food so that the people of Egypt would have something to eat.
- Joseph's brothers came to Egypt to buy food.
- Joseph's brothers didn't recognize him, but Joseph knew who they were. He didn't want them to know who he was yet.
- Pharaoh's bad dreams had predicted a famine—a time when food would be hard to find. When Pharaoh put Joseph in charge, he prepared by storing food. Joseph's family needed food, so they went to Egypt to purchase grain. Joseph recognized his brothers, but they did not recognize Joseph. He didn't want them to know who he was just yet.

APPLY

Joseph had been through lots of hard times, but God had used them to place Joseph where he could help lots of people. Joseph followed God when good things and bad things happened. By following God, Joseph would have a chance to see his family again. Help three of Joseph's brothers find their way to the healthy grain.

RESPOND

PRAY: Heavenly Father, please help me to always follow You, whether good things or bad things happen.

HIGHLIGHT

OLDER KIDS: Genesis 45:3-8
YOUNGER KIDS: Genesis 45:3-5
MEMORY VERSE: Romans 8:28

EXPLAIN

- Joseph told his brothers who he was, and they were afraid he was angry with them.
- Joseph told his brothers not to be afraid. He was not angry, and he had forgiven them.
- Joseph told his brothers that God had planned for him to be in Egypt so he could help save his own family and other people when there wasn't anything to eat.
- Joseph finally told his brothers who he was. They were afraid Joseph would be angry with them because they had sold him as a slave. Joseph wasn't angry—he had forgiven them. Joseph realized it was God's plan for him to be in Egypt. God had placed Joseph in a position to help save not only the people of Egypt, but also his own family.

APPLY

Joseph showed forgiveness and compassion to his brothers. God shows us forgiveness and compassion through Jesus. Even though we have sinned, God loves us and made a way for us to be forgiven through Jesus. Discuss: Have you ever forgiven someone for something they did to you? Was it easy or hard?

RESPOND

PRAY: God, thank You for showing compassion and forgiveness to me. Please help me to show forgiveness and compassion to others.

HIGHLIGHT

OLDER KIDS: Genesis 46:1-6
YOUNGER KIDS: Genesis 46:5-6
MEMORY VERSE: Romans 8:28

EXPLAIN

- Israel (Jacob, Joseph's father) left his home and went to Egypt with all his family, animals, and everything he owned.
- Pharaoh met Joseph's brothers and father, and Pharaoh told Joseph to give them the best part of the land for their home.
- Pharaoh also trusted Joseph to put his brothers in charge of Pharaoh's animals.
- Because Joseph was in charge of Egypt under Pharaoh, he was able to bring his family to live in Egypt. Jacob brought his entire family, their animals, and all their stuff to live in the best part of Egypt. Pharaoh even trusted Joseph enough to put his brothers in charge of Pharaoh's animals.

APPLY

Because Joseph followed God in good times and in bad times, God provided a way for Joseph's family and for the people of Egypt to be rescued when they had nothing to eat. God provided a rescue from sin for us through Jesus. Draw a line on the map that shows the journey Jacob and his family made to move from Canaan to Egypt.

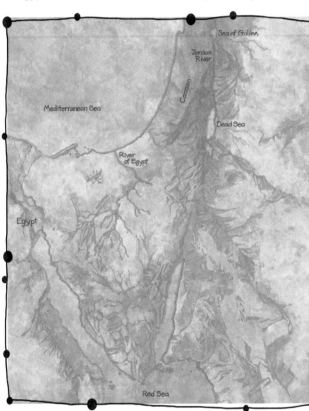

RESPOND

PRAY: Heavenly Father, thank You for providing a rescue for us through Jesus.

 HIGHLIGHT

OLDER KIDS: Genesis 48:8-12
YOUNGER KIDS: Genesis 48:8-9
MEMORY VERSE: Genesis 50:20

 **EXPLAIN**

- When Joseph's brothers sold him as a slave and lied to their father, Jacob thought he would never see Joseph again, but God brought them back together.
- Joseph took his sons to meet their grandfather, Jacob. Jacob was old and couldn't see well, but he was happy to meet his grandsons.
- Jacob made sure Joseph and his sons received the blessings God had promised their family.
- Not only did Jacob get to see Joseph again, he got to see Joseph's sons, too. Jacob gave Joseph and his sons a special blessing so the promise God had given their family included them.

 APPLY

Jacob adopted Joseph's sons into their family because he wanted God's promise for their family to include them. Jesus lived a life without sin and took our punishment for sin so we can be adopted into God's family and receive His blessings. Look at the pictures below each box and write the first letter of each object in the box.

RESPOND

PRAY: Jesus, thank You for taking the punishment for my sins so I can be adopted into God's family.

 HIGHLIGHT

OLDER KIDS: Genesis 50:15-21
YOUNGER KIDS: Genesis 50:19-21
MEMORY VERSE: Genesis 50:20

 EXPLAIN

- After Jacob died, Joseph's brothers feared Joseph might want to repay them for selling him into slavery.
- Joseph wasn't angry with his brothers. He had forgiven them a long time ago.
- God used the cruel things Joseph's brothers had done to make good things happen for lots of people.
- Joseph's brothers were afraid of being punished after their father died, but Joseph was not upset with his brothers. He saw that God used his past to help others.

 APPLY

God is always working to make His plan happen. Even when people do mean things, God can use them for good.

Write this week's memory verse in the box.

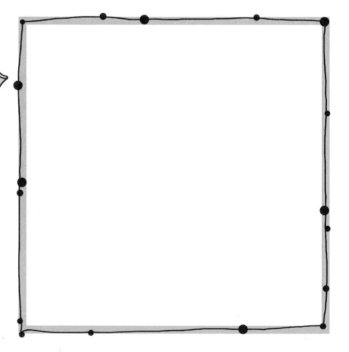

 RESPOND

PRAY: Heavenly Father, thank You for always working to make Your plan happen, even when people do mean things.

HIGHLIGHT

OLDER KIDS: Exodus 1:8-10; 2:5-10
YOUNGER KIDS: Exodus 2:5-10
MEMORY VERSE: Genesis 50:20

EXPLAIN

- A long time passed, and a new Pharaoh was ruling Egypt. He was afraid there were too many Israelites, so he ordered that Israelite boy babies should be killed.
- Moses' mother hid him in the river so Pharaoh's men wouldn't kill him. Moses' sister watched to see what would happen to him.
- Pharaoh's daughter found Moses and felt sorry for him. She asked Moses' mother to help care for him while he was a baby. Then, Pharaoh's daughter raised Moses as her own child.
- A long time after Joseph helped save the people of Egypt, a new Pharaoh was in charge. He was afraid of the Israelites and didn't want them to fight against him in a war. Pharaoh's daughter found him and had Moses' mother help care for him. Then Pharaoh's daughter raised Moses as her own son.

APPLY

God had a plan for Moses to bring the Israelites out of Egypt and back to their land. When Moses had grown into a man and was working as a shepherd, God used a burning bush to call Moses to rescue the Israelites. God is always working to carry out His plan. Draw a picture of baby Moses and his basket in the reeds below.

RESPOND

PRAY: Heavenly Father, thank You for always working to carry out Your plan.

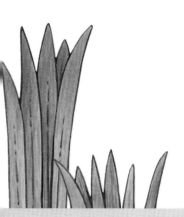

HIGHLIGHT

OLDER KIDS: Exodus 4:10-15
YOUNGER KIDS: Exodus 4:10-12
MEMORY VERSE: Genesis 50:20

EXPLAIN

- God spoke to Moses out of a burning bush. God told Moses to rescue the Israelites from Egypt, but Moses was afraid.
- Moses didn't speak well and tried to use it as an excuse not to do what God wanted him to do.
- Moses' brother, Aaron, could speak well. God used Aaron to help Moses carry out His plan.
- Moses had been called by God to rescue the Israelites from slavery in Egypt, but he was afraid. Moses didn't speak well and tried to use his weakness as an excuse. Moses' brother was a good speaker, so God used him to help Moses complete the task.

APPLY

Sometimes God calls us to do things we are afraid to do or don't think we are able to do. God will provide everything we need to carry out His plan. Moses didn't think he could speak well. Do you ever feel tongue-tied? Figure out which kid isn't afraid to speak up by starting in the center and working your way backward out of the tongue-tangle.

RESPOND

PRAY: God, thank You for providing everything I need to carry out Your plan. Help me to trust You and not to be afraid.

HIGHLIGHT

OLDER KIDS: Exodus 6:6-9
YOUNGER KIDS: Exodus 6:6-7
MEMORY VERSE: Genesis 50:20

EXPLAIN

- Moses went to Pharaoh and told him that God wanted him to let the Israelites go. Pharaoh was angry and made the Israelites work harder.
- Moses told the Israelites about God's promise to free them from slavery in Egypt and return them to the land He had promised to Abraham, Isaac, and Jacob.
- The Israelites were very tired from working for Pharaoh, and they didn't want to hear what Moses had to say.
- Moses and Aaron went to tell Pharaoh that God wanted him to free the Israelites. Pharaoh was angry with their words, so he made the Israelites work harder. Moses went to the Israelites and told them about God's promise to free them from Egypt and return them to their homeland. Because they were so tired from working for Pharaoh, they didn't want to listen.

APPLY

God did not forget His promise to Abraham, Isaac, and Jacob. Even though the Israelites were in slavery, God had a plan to rescue them from Egypt. Discuss: Why do you think it was hard for the Israelites to believe Moses?

RESPOND

PRAY: Heavenly Father, thank You for always remembering Your promises and working to carry them out.

HIGHLIGHT

OLDER KIDS: Exodus 9:1-7
YOUNGER KIDS: Exodus 9:1-3
MEMORY VERSE: John 1:29

 ## EXPLAIN

- Moses kept asking Pharaoh to let God's people go, but he kept saying no.
- God sent a plague on Pharaoh and the people of Egypt every time Pharaoh said no to Moses.
- The Egyptians' animals died, but the Israelites' animals were not hurt.
- Moses and Aaron kept going back to Pharaoh, asking him to let the Israelites go, and he kept saying no. Each time Pharaoh said no, God sent a plague. During the fifth plague, the Egyptians' animals died, but God spared the animals of the Israelites. Still, Pharaoh would not let the Israelites go.

APPLY

God used the plagues to show the Egyptians and the Israelites that He is the one true God and is in charge of everything. Complete the Plague Sudoku puzzle. Each row, column, and six-square grid should have only one of each of the six plagues shown here (darkness, dying fish in the Nile, diseased livestock, biting insects, fiery hail, frogs). Draw the plague that is missing from each blank.

 ## RESPOND

PRAY: God, thank You for being the one true God and for being in charge of everything.

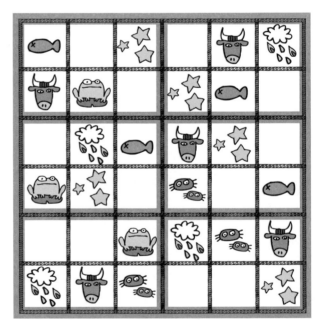

HIGHLIGHT

OLDER KIDS: Exodus 11:1,4-8
YOUNGER KIDS: Exodus 11:1,4-5
MEMORY VERSE: John 1:29

EXPLAIN

- God sent one last plague so Pharaoh would decide to let the Israelites go.
- God had Moses tell Pharaoh He would kill every firstborn in the land except for those of the Israelites. We call this event the *Passover*.
- God said that after this last plague, Pharaoh would bow down to Him and would tell the Israelites to leave.
- God sent the tenth plague so Pharaoh would let the Israelites go. Moses told Pharaoh that God would kill every firstborn of the Egyptians but not of the Israelites. God declared that after the Passover, Pharaoh would bow down to Him and tell the Israelites to leave Egypt.

 APPLY

God provided protection for the Israelites during the plagues. God's plan was not only for the Israelites to be rescued, but also for everyone to know He is the one true God. With a parent, talk about a time God protected you or a member of your family.

 **RESPOND**

PRAY: God, thank You for protecting us and for showing us that You are the one true God.

 HIGHLIGHT

OLDER KIDS: Exodus 12:12-14
YOUNGER KIDS: Exodus 12:12-13
MEMORY VERSE: John 1:29

EXPLAIN

- God gave the Israelites instructions so they would be protected during the tenth plague that we now call Passover.
- The Israelites were told to put the blood of a sacrifice on the doors of their homes. God would pass over their house, and no one in their homes would be hurt.
- God instructed the Israelites always to remember the day of Passover in celebration of how He brought them out of slavery in Egypt.
- God wanted the Israelites to be protected during the tenth plague, so He instructed them to put the blood of a sacrifice on the door posts of their houses. He would pass over the house, and no one would be hurt. God wanted the Israelites always to remember the day of Passover and celebrate how He rescued them from Egypt.

 APPLY

During Passover, God used the blood of a sacrificed sheep or goat to rescue the Israelites from Egypt. God sent Jesus to be the sacrifice to rescue us from our sin. Fill in the blanks from John 1:29.

_____ NEXT DAY _____ SAW JESUS

COMING _____ HIM AND SAID, "_____ THE

LAMB OF GOD _____ THE SIN OF THE WORLD."

 **RESPOND**

PRAY: Heavenly Father, thank You for sending Jesus to rescue me from sin.

 HIGHLIGHT

OLDER KIDS: Exodus 14:21-28
YOUNGER KIDS: Exodus 14:21-22
MEMORY VERSE: John 1:29

 EXPLAIN

- After Pharaoh freed the Israelites, he changed his mind and wanted them to come back. He sent his army after them.
- God parted the water of the Red Sea so the Israelites could walk across on dry land. They all crossed safely!
- The Egyptian army tried to cross the Red Sea behind the Israelites, but God let the water go back to its place. All the Egyptians who were chasing the Israelites died.
- The Israelites were finally leaving Egypt, but Pharaoh changed his mind and chased after them. God parted the water of the Red Sea so the Israelites could walk across on dry land. When the Egyptians tried to chase the Israelites through the Red Sea, God let the water go back to its place, and the Egyptian army drowned.

APPLY

God provided a way for the Israelites to escape Pharaoh's army. He also showed the Israelites that they could trust and believe in Him. Circle 8 items the Israelites did NOT take along as they escaped Pharaoh's army.

 RESPOND

PRAY: Heavenly Father, thank You that I can trust and believe in You.

HIGHLIGHT

OLDER KIDS: Exodus 16:11-15
YOUNGER KIDS: Exodus 16:11-12
MEMORY VERSE: John 1:29

EXPLAIN

- The Israelites were in the wilderness and were unhappy about not having enough food to eat.
- God told Moses He would provide meat and bread for the Israelites so they would know He is God.
- God sent quail (small birds) and manna (bread) for the Israelites to eat so they would not be hungry.
- The Israelites were hungry and upset in the wilderness without enough food, so God provided quail and manna so that the Israelites would not be hungry and would know He is God.

APPLY

God provided food for the Israelites, and God provides for us! Think about how God provides for you as you match the questions and answers in the spaghetti maze.

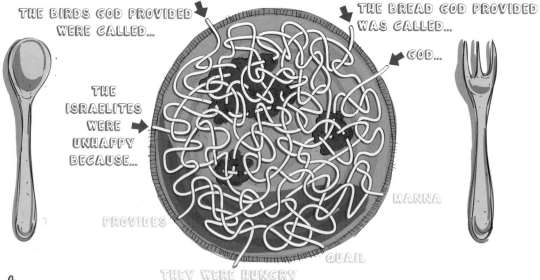

THE BIRDS GOD PROVIDED WERE CALLED...

THE BREAD GOD PROVIDED WAS CALLED...

GOD...

THE ISRAELITES WERE UNHAPPY BECAUSE...

MANNA

PROVIDES

QUAIL

THEY WERE HUNGRY

RESPOND

PRAY: Heavenly Father, thank You for providing for me.

 HIGHLIGHT

OLDER KIDS: Exodus 20:1-17
YOUNGER KIDS: Exodus 20:1-3
MEMORY VERSE: Galatians 5:14

EXPLAIN

- The Israelites needed rules to live by so they could follow God.
- God gave Moses the Ten Commandments for the Israelites to live by.
- God's commandments helped the Israelites remember they needed God.
- The Israelites needed rules to live by so they could follow God and know how to live as His chosen people. God gave Moses the Ten Commandments to help the Israelites live by God's rules and also to help them remember that they needed God.

APPLY

God promised Abraham to make his offspring into a great nation, and He had done that. Now the people needed rules to follow so they could know how to live for God. The Ten Commandments still help us follow God. Draw a line to connect each piece of the tablet to its proper place.

 RESPOND

PRAY: God, thank You for giving us the Ten Commandments to help us follow You.

HIGHLIGHT

OLDER KIDS: Exodus 25:1-9
YOUNGER KIDS: Exodus 25:8-9
MEMORY VERSE: Galatians 5:14

EXPLAIN

- God told Moses to take an offering from the people for Him.
- God gave Moses instructions to build a tabernacle using the offerings people gave.
- God wanted the Israelites to build a tabernacle so that He could be with them all the time.
- God told Moses to collect an offering from the people. The offering included things such as gold and silver, jewelry, fabrics, wood, and spices. God gave Moses instructions to use those offerings to build a tabernacle so He could live with the Israelites all the time.

 APPLY

God told the Israelites to build a tabernacle so He could live with them. God wants to be with His people. After Jesus went to heaven, God sent the Holy Spirit so He can be with us all the time. Unscramble the letters of offerings and match them to their correct picture.

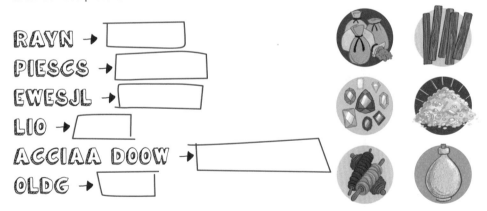

RAYN →
PIESCS →
EWESJL →
LIO →
ACCIAA DOOW →
OLDG →

 **RESPOND**

PRAY: Heavenly Father, thank You for wanting to be with us all the time and for sending the Holy Spirit.

 HIGHLIGHT

OLDER KIDS: Exodus 26:31-35
YOUNGER KIDS: Exodus 26:33
MEMORY VERSE: Galatians 5:14

EXPLAIN

- The tabernacle was a big tent used for worship gatherings.
- The veil was a big curtain that separated the people from God because they could not be in His presence because of their sin.
- God's instructions were very specific. He wanted things to be a certain way in the tabernacle.
- God's tabernacle was a big tent where the Israelites worshiped Him. The veil separated the people from God because the people could not be in God's presence.

APPLY

The people of Israel could not be in God's presence. Later, when Jesus died on the cross, the veil in the tabernacle was torn. Because Jesus paid the price for our sins, we can talk directly to God. Color the tabernacle curtain blue, purple, and red.

 RESPOND

PRAY: Heavenly Father, thank You for sending Jesus to pay the price for our sins so we can talk directly to You.

HIGHLIGHT

OLDER KIDS: Exodus 29:38-42
YOUNGER KIDS: Exodus 29:38-39
MEMORY VERSE: Galatians 5:14

EXPLAIN

- God gave specific instructions for the people's sacrifices.
- God asked the people to give the best they had as their sacrifice.
- The people were to give their best to God every day.
- God gave detailed instructions for the people's sacrifices. He wanted their very best. They were to give sacrifices to God two times every day.

APPLY

God wants us to give our best to Him. Giving God our best shows our obedience and thankfulness to Him for giving us His best in Jesus Christ. With a parent, discuss what it means to give God your best.

RESPOND

PRAY: Heavenly Father, thank You for giving us Your best. Help me to always give You my best.

HIGHLIGHT

OLDER KIDS: Exodus 31:12-13,16-17
YOUNGER KIDS: Exodus 31:16-17
MEMORY VERSE: Galatians 5:14

EXPLAIN

- God wanted the Israelites to set aside a day of rest called the *Sabbath* as a covenant (promise) between Him and the Israelites.
- God instructed the Israelites to rest on the Sabbath and to dedicate the day to Him.
- Holding the Sabbath as a day of rest helps us to remember that God made everything in six days and then rested on the seventh and final day.
- God instructed the Israelites to dedicate the Sabbath to Him. The Sabbath is a covenant between God and His people to remind us that God rested on the seventh day.

APPLY

God wants us to set aside time to rest and to spend time focused on Him. Using the Morse Code key, decode the following word:

RESPOND

PRAY: God, thank You for giving us time for rest and focusing on You.

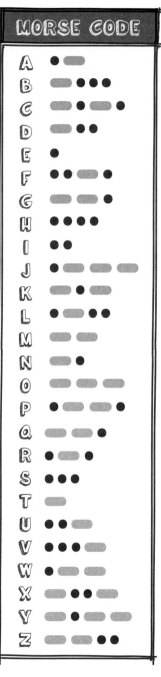

MORSE CODE

A • ▬
B ▬ • • •
C ▬ • ▬ •
D ▬ • •
E •
F • • ▬ •
G ▬ ▬ •
H • • • •
I • •
J • ▬ ▬ ▬
K ▬ • ▬
L • ▬ • •
M ▬ ▬
N ▬ •
O ▬ ▬ ▬
P • ▬ ▬ •
Q ▬ ▬ • ▬
R • ▬ •
S • • •
T ▬
U • • ▬
V • • • ▬
W • ▬ ▬
X ▬ • • ▬
Y ▬ • ▬ ▬
Z ▬ ▬ • •

HIGHLIGHT

OLDER KIDS: Exodus 32:1,7-8
YOUNGER KIDS: Exodus 32:1,7-8
MEMORY VERSES: Matthew 22:37-38

EXPLAIN

- Moses was up on Mount Sinai, where God gave him the Ten Commandments.
- The Israelites convinced Aaron to make an idol—a golden calf—for them to worship instead of God.
- God saw what the Israelites were doing and was angry. He sent Moses down to stop them.
- While Moses was up on Mount Sinai with God, the people of Israel approached Aaron. Moses was taking longer getting the Ten Commandments than the people thought he should, so they convinced Aaron to make a golden calf for them to worship instead of God. God was angry when He saw the people's idol they were worshiping. He told Moses to go down the mountain and stop them.

APPLY

The Israelites sinned by worshiping a golden calf. It is a sin to make anything more important than God. With a parent, discuss what it means to make something more important than God.

RESPOND

PRAY: Heavenly Father, help me never to make anything more important than You.

 **HIGHLIGHT**

OLDER KIDS: Exodus 34:1-4
YOUNGER KIDS: Exodus 34:1-2
MEMORY VERSES: Matthew 22:37-38

 EXPLAIN

- When Moses saw the Israelites worshiping the golden calf, he angrily threw down the tablets God had written the Ten Commandments on and broke them.
- God gave Moses instructions to make two new tablets. God was going to write His commandments again on these tablets.
- Moses climbed Mount Sinai with the new tablets, just like God told him to do.
- When Moses came down the mountain, he saw the Israelites worshiping their golden calf idol. In his anger, Moses threw down the Ten Commandments, and they broke. God instructed Moses to make new tablets and bring them back up to Mount Sinai so He could write His commandments again.

 APPLY

God forgave the Israelites for thier sin against Him. God forgives us when we ask Him to forgive us. Using the clues below, construct the story of God giving Moses the Ten Commandments.

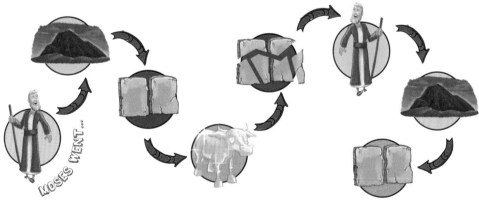

 **RESPOND**

PRAY: Heavenly Father, thank You for forgiving me when I ask.

HIGHLIGHT

OLDER KIDS: Exodus 40:34-38
YOUNGER KIDS: Exodus 40:34-35
MEMORY VERSES: Matthew 22:37-38

EXPLAIN

- God gave the Israelites instructions for how to build the tabernacle so He could stay with His people.
- Once the tabernacle's construction was finished, God's glory (His presence) filled it!
- God's sign for the people was a cloud over the tabernacle. If the cloud stayed put, the Israelites were also to stay. If the cloud moved, it was time for them to move as well.
- The Israelites obeyed God's instructions as they built the tabernacle. God's glory filled it. God gave the people a sign by the cloud. If the cloud stayed, the people stayed where they were. If the cloud moved, they were to follow it.

 APPLY

God told the Israelites to build the tabernacle because He wanted to be with them all the time. God loves us like He loved the Israelites. When does God want to be with us? Decode the answer by writing the first letter of each picture in the box.

COLOR

 **RESPOND**

PRAY: God, thank You for loving me and for wanting to be with me all the time.

HIGHLIGHT

OLDER KIDS: Leviticus 9:22-24
YOUNGER KIDS: Leviticus 9:22-23
MEMORY VERSES: Matthew 22:37-38

 ## EXPLAIN

- The priests offered sacrifices to God to atone, or cover, the people's sins.
- God spoke to the people through the priests.
- Priests talked to God for the people.
- The priests offered sacrifices to God to pay for the Iraelites' sins. God communicated with His people through the priests, and the priests talked to God for the people.

 ## APPLY

The Israelites needed a priest to talk to God for them. Jesus came to be our High Priest and to make one enormous sacrifice for us. Because of our High Priest's sacrifice, we can now talk to God ourselves. Look at each row of old telephones and circle the shadow that matches the original.

 ## RESPOND

PRAY: Heavenly Father, thank You for sending Jesus to be my High Priest so I can talk to You.

HIGHLIGHT
OLDER KIDS: Leviticus 16:15-16
YOUNGER KIDS: Leviticus 16:16
MEMORY VERSES: Matthew 22:37-38

EXPLAIN
- God gave Moses specific instructions for how the priests were to make sacrifices for the people's sins.
- *Sacrifices* are gifts people give to God.
- Sacrifices could be different things—grain or bread, money, or animals.
- God wants to be with His people, but because He is holy, He cannot be around sin. Sacrifices were gifts people gave to God so they may be forgiven of their sins. God gave the priests detailed instructions on how to make sacrifices for the people's sins.

APPLY
The priests offered sacrifices as a way to ask God for forgiveness of the people's sins. Jesus came to be our ultimate sacrifice, once and for all, so we can be forgiven of our sins. Circle the things priests might have to sacrifice for the forgiveness of sins. Cross out the pictures that would not be an Old Testament sacrifice.

RESPOND
PRAY: Heavenly Father, thank You for sending Jesus to be the sacrifice for my sins.

HIGHLIGHT

OLDER KIDS: Leviticus 23:1-3
YOUNGER KIDS: Leviticus 23:3
MEMORY VERSE: Deuteronomy 31:8

EXPLAIN

- God gave Moses specific instructions for the Israelites to set aside special times for rest and worship.
- God's day of rest is called the *Sabbath*.
- The Israelites were forbidden to do any work on the Sabbath.
- The Sabbath was for rest, and the people were not allowed to do any work on that day. The people followed God's example of resting on the seventh day of creation.

APPLY

We should set aside time for rest and to worship God wherever we live. Decode the puzzle to find out what the Sabbath is for in the last box.

RESPOND

PRAY: Heavenly Father, thank You for giving us times of rest and worship.

START WITH THE WORD

TENT

REPLACE THE **N** WITH **X**

REPLACE THE FIRST **T** WITH **N**

REPLACE THE **X** WITH **S**

REPLACE THE **N** WITH **T**

REPLACE THE FIRST **T** WITH **B**

REPLACE THE **B** WITH **R**

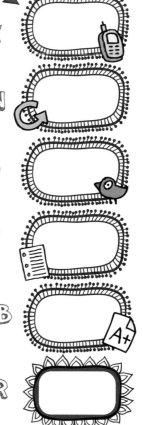

HIGHLIGHT · EXPLAIN · APPLY · RESPOND   READING #46   51

HIGHLIGHT

OLDER KIDS: Leviticus 26:3-8
YOUNGER KIDS: Leviticus 26:3-4
MEMORY VERSE: Deuteronomy 31:8

EXPLAIN

- God reminded the Israelites to obey Him.
- God assured the Israelites that obedience would bring the peace of God's presence.
- God warned the Israelites if they disobeyed, they would experience difficult times and be punished.
- God reminded the Israelites to obey His commands, reminding them that obedience would bring peace and harvest but disobedience would bring harm. God wanted to remind them of the covenant He made with Abraham. Since God is just, He also warned the Israelites that their disobedience would lead to punishment.

APPLY

God doesn't only do good things when we are obedient. Because of Jesus' obedience on the cross, God's blessings do not depend on our obedience. Fill in the blanks to reveal the memory verse, Deuteronomy 31:8:

_____

BEFORE YOU _____ BE WITH YOU; HE WILL

_____ .

DO NOT _____ .

RESPOND

PRAY: Jesus, thank You for Your obedience on the cross.

HIGHLIGHT

OLDER KIDS: Numbers 11:1-3
YOUNGER KIDS: Numbers 11:1-2
MEMORY VERSE: Deuteronomy 31:8

EXPLAIN

- The Israelites complained to God because their lives came with hardships.
- God was angry at the Israelites for complaining, so He burned the outside of their camp.
- The Israelites were scared, so they begged Moses to pray to God for the people. Moses prayed, and God's fire went away, but the Israelites continued to complain.
- The Israelites were unhappy and complained to God. God was angry at the Israelites for their complaints, and His fire burned up the outside of the camp. Moses prayed to God for the people, and God's fire went away.

APPLY

Moses prayed to God on behalf of the people. Because Jesus paid the price for our sins, we can talk directly to God, and He will listen. With a parent, discuss how we talk to God. How does God talk to us?

RESPOND

PRAY: Jesus, thank You for paying the price for my sins so I can talk to God.

 **HIGHLIGHT**

OLDER KIDS: Numbers 13:26-29
YOUNGER KIDS: Numbers 13:26-28
MEMORY VERSE: Deuteronomy 31:8

 EXPLAIN

- Moses sent twelve men into the land of Canaan, which God had promised to the Israelites. The twelve spies went to see what Canaan was like.
- When the men returned from Canaan, they told Moses that the land was wonderful, but the people that lived there were scary and would be hard to defeat.
- Caleb and Joshua were two of the spies. They were not afraid. They trusted in God and were sure that Canaan could be conquered.
- Moses chose twelve men to survey God's promised land. The men came back telling Moses about all the wonderful things in the promised land. Ten of the men were afraid of the people who lived in Canaan, but Joshua and Caleb were not afraid.

APPLY

We do not need to be afraid when we trust in God because He is always with us. Place a check mark next to the items you are sometimes afraid of. Remember that God is always with you.

Bats · Storms · Dentist · Scary movies · Tests · Gross Stuff · Death · Snakes · Flying · Spiders · Weapons · Shots

 **RESPOND**

PRAY: God, thank You for always being with me.

HIGHLIGHT

OLDER KIDS: Numbers 16:46-50
YOUNGER KIDS: Numbers 16:47-48
MEMORY VERSE: Deuteronomy 31:8

 # EXPLAIN

- Because the Israelites had sinned, God sent a plague to punish them.
- Moses and Aaron made atonement for (asked God to forgive) the people's sin.
- God stopped the plague, but many people had died already.
- The Israelites had disobeyed God, so He sent a plague to punish them for their sins. Moses and Aaron asked God to forgive the people for their sins. God stopped the plague, but not before thousands of people died.

 # APPLY

The Israelites had a sin problem. We have a sin problem too, but Jesus paid the price for our sins, so we can be forgiven. Find and circle the highlighted words in the word search.

RESPOND

PRAY: Jesus, thank You for paying the price for my sin so I can be forgiven.

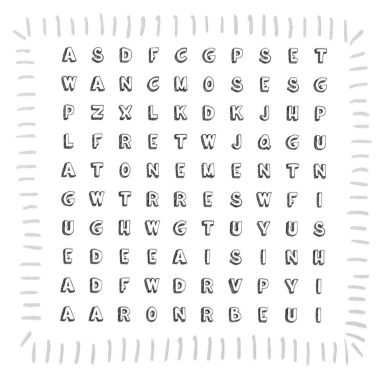

WEEK 11
DAY 1

HIGHLIGHT

OLDER KIDS: Numbers 20:7-11
YOUNGER KIDS: Numbers 20:10-11
MEMORY VERSE: Deuteronomy 4:7

EXPLAIN

- The Israelites complained because there wasn't enough water.
- God gave Moses and Aaron instructions for how to get water for the people.
- Moses sinned by not following God's instructions.
- The Israelites were groaning because there wasn't enough water for the people and their animals. God told Moses and Aaron He would provide water and gave them instructions to get the water. Instead of speaking to the rock like God said, Moses hit the rock with his staff. God still provided the water, but Moses and Aaron were punished for their disobedience by not getting to go into the promised land.

APPLY

Everyone sins. Even Moses sinned. The only person who has ever lived without sin is Jesus. Jesus took the punishment for our sins even though He had never sinned. Follow the instructions carefully in order to make it through this maze of signs.

RESPOND

PRAY: Jesus, thank You for taking the punishment for my sin.

HIGHLIGHT

OLDER KIDS: Numbers 34:13-15
YOUNGER KIDS: Numbers 34:13
MEMORY VERSE: Deuteronomy 4:7

EXPLAIN

- The Israelites had been in the wilderness for a long time.
- The Israelites were finally getting ready to cross into the promised land.
- God divided the land for each of the twelve tribes of Israel.
- They were finally getting ready to cross into Canaan, the promised land. Each tribe was getting its own piece of land, divided the way God instructed.

APPLY

God promised Moses that He would lead the Israelites to the land He had promised to Abraham, Isaac, and Jacob. Even though it took a long time, God kept His promise and provided for the Israelites. Follow the letters to complete the maze and find your way to the promised land.

RESPOND

PRAY: Heavenly Father, thank You for always keeping Your promises.

HIGHLIGHT

OLDER KIDS: Deuteronomy 2:2-7
YOUNGER KIDS: Deuteronomy 2:7
MEMORY VERSE: Deuteronomy 4:7

EXPLAIN

- The Book of Deuteronomy, written by Moses, reminds us of what happened while the Israelites were wandering in the wilderness.
- Moses told the Israelites stories to help them remember the things that happened.
- Moses reminded the Israelites God had been faithful in taking care of them.
- The Book of Deuteronomy gives us an account of what happened to the Israelites as they wandered in the wilderness. Moses told the Israelites stories to help them remember the things that happened. Moses reminded the people that God had faithfully cared for them the whole time.

APPLY

God was faithful to take care of the Israelites, and He will be faithful to take care of us. With a parent, brainstorm together a time that God was faithful and took care of you.

RESPOND

PRAY: God, thank You for being faithful to take care of me.

HIGHLIGHT

OLDER KIDS: Deuteronomy 4:1-5
YOUNGER KIDS: Deuteronomy 4:1-2
MEMORY VERSE: Deuteronomy 4:7

EXPLAIN

- Moses reminded the Israelites of the laws God had given them to follow so they could enter the promised land.
- Moses reminded the Israelites that they had been taught everything they needed to know to follow God faithfully.
- Moses also reminded them that disobedience leads to destruction.
- Moses reminded the Israelites of God's laws and the importance of following them. Moses had taught everything they needed to know to follow God. Moses reminded them to obey.

APPLY

It was important for the Israelites to follow God's commands, and it is important for us, too. Write this week's memory verse in the box.

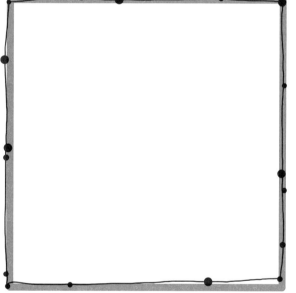

RESPOND

PRAY:

Heavenly Father, thank You for giving us instructions to follow. Please help me follow Your instructions.

 HIGHLIGHT

OLDER KIDS: Deuteronomy 6:4-9
YOUNGER KIDS: Deuteronomy 6:5-6
MEMORY VERSE: Deuteronomy 4:7

EXPLAIN

- Moses instructed the people to love God with all their heart, soul, and strength.
- Moses also told them it was important to teach their kids this command.
- This commandment to love God is so important that the people were told to make signs and symbols on their own bodies in remembrance of this command. They were told to write it on their doorposts, too!
- Moses told the Israelites to love God with all their heart, soul, and strength, and to teach their kids to love God this way, too. This command was so important that the people displayed signs on their bodies and doors so they would always remember God's command.

 APPLY

We are supposed to love God with all our heart, soul, and strength. Using both words and pictures, design a sign that can help you remember to love God.

 RESPOND

PRAY: Heavenly Father, thank You for loving me. Help me always to love You and put You first.

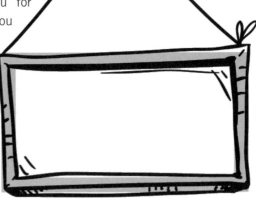

HIGHLIGHT

OLDER KIDS: Deuteronomy 8:1-6
YOUNGER KIDS: Deuteronomy 8:1-2
MEMORY VERSE: Joshua 1:9

EXPLAIN

- Moses continued talking to the Israelites, urging them to follow God's commands.
- Moses always reminded the Israelites how God had taken care of them.
- Moses reminded that God used hard times to draw them closer to Him.
- Moses talked to the Israelites about following God and His commands. Following His commands was necessary for the Israelites to enter the promised land. God had always taken care of them, and He used times of difficulty to remind them how much they needed Him.

APPLY

It is good to remember God's commands and the ways He has taken care of us. With a parent, answer and discuss the following question: Why do you think Moses spent so much time reminding the Israelites to follow God's commands?

RESPOND

PRAY: Heavenly Father, thank You for Your commands and for taking care of me.

 **HIGHLIGHT**

OLDER KIDS: Deuteronomy 30:11,19-20
YOUNGER KIDS: Deuteronomy 30:20
MEMORY VERSE: Joshua 1:9

 EXPLAIN

- God's commandments are never too hard for people to obey.
- We have the choice whether to follow God's commands or to disobey Him.
- Moses wanted the people to choose to follow God. Choosing Him brings life and blessings, and not choosing Him brings disaster.
- We can choose whether to follow God's commands or not to obey. Moses wanted the Israelites to follow God's commands because He promised that obedience to Him would give the people prosperity in the promised land.

 APPLY

Following God is not too hard to do, but we must decide every day whether or not we are going to follow Him. Follow these commands:

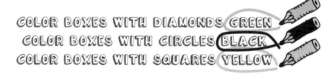

COLOR BOXES WITH DIAMONDS GREEN
COLOR BOXES WITH CIRCLES BLACK
COLOR BOXES WITH SQUARES YELLOW

 **RESPOND**

PRAY: God, thank You for giving me the choice to follow You. Please help me to follow You and to obey Your commands.

HIGHLIGHT

OLDER KIDS: Deuteronomy 34:5,9-12
YOUNGER KIDS: Deuteronomy 34:5,9
MEMORY VERSE: Joshua 1:9

EXPLAIN

- After Moses saw the promised land, God told Moses it was time for him to die.
- Moses died, just as God said he would, and Joshua took over as leader of the Israelites.
- The Israelites never had another leader like Moses. Moses had a special relationship with God.
- God told Moses it was almost time for him to die. Moses died in the land of Moab, as God had said he would, and Joshua became the new leader of the Israelites. Israel never had another leader like Moses—he was special because he had talked face-to-face with God, and God had done many things through Moses.

APPLY

Moses was a special leader, but he couldn't lead the Israelites forever. God's plan often includes changes. Write Joshua 1:9 in the shape to the right.

RESPOND

PRAY: Heavenly Father, thank You for including change in Your plans.

HIGHLIGHT

OLDER KIDS: Joshua 1:6-9
YOUNGER KIDS: Joshua 1:8-9
MEMORY VERSE: Joshua 1:9

MARITIME FLAGS

A
B
C
D
E
F
G
H
I
J
K
L
M
N
O
P
Q
R
S
T
U
V
W
X
Y
Z

EXPLAIN

- Joshua had just become the leader of all the Israelites. It was a big job!
- Moses had taught Joshua to follow God's commands. God told Joshua that if he followed the commands, he would be a successful leader of God's people.
- God told Joshua not to be afraid because He would be with Joshua wherever he led the people of Israel.
- Moses died and Joshua became the new leader of all the Israelites. The role as leader was a very important job! God told Joshua to follow His commands as Moses taught him to do. God did not want Joshua to be afraid and told Joshua He would be with him wherever he went.

APPLY

God is always with us and does not want us to be afraid. Be strong and courageous! Decode the message using the Maritime Flags Code.

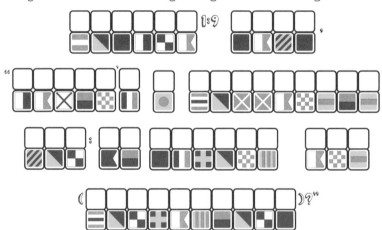

RESPOND

PRAY: Heavenly Father, thank You for being with me so I don't have to be afraid.

 **HIGHLIGHT**

OLDER KIDS: Joshua 4:1-7
YOUNGER KIDS: Joshua 4:4-7
MEMORY VERSE: Joshua 1:9

 EXPLAIN

- The Israelites finally crossed the Jordan River into the promised land, and God held the water back so they could walk across on dry land.
- God instructed Joshua to order one man from each of the twelve tribes of Israel to take a stone from the river.
- These twelve large stones were set up as a sign of Israel's entry into the promised land, so that the people could tell their kids about all God had done.
- The Israelites were finally crossing the Jordan River into the promised land. God held back the water so they could walk on dry land! Joshua had one man from each tribe remove a stone from the river—twelve stones in all. The stones were set up as a memorial so the people could remember and tell their kids about all God had done for them.

 APPLY

God wants us to remember the things He has done for us. In the spaces below, list three things God has done for you that you would like to remember.

RESPOND

PRAY: God, please help me to remember the things You have done for me.

HIGHLIGHT

OLDER KIDS: Joshua 6:2-5
YOUNGER KIDS: Joshua 6:3-5
MEMORY VERSE: Joshua 24:14

EXPLAIN

- Joshua and the Israelites were in the promised land getting ready to take over the city of Jericho.
- God gave Joshua specific instructions on how to conquer Jericho. They would march around the walls, and the walls would fall down.
- God told Joshua that He would fight the battle for them.
- After Moses' death, Joshua had led the Israelites into the promised land. The people were preparing to attack the city of Jericho, which was controlled by their enemies. God gave Joshua very specific instructions to march around the walls of Jericho and they would fall down. He promised He would win the battle for them.

APPLY

It is always best to follow God's instructions, even though they seem strange to us at first. We don't always know or understand God's plan, but He always does! With a parent, talk about a time you received instructions you thought didn't make sense. Who gave them to you? What did you do?

RESPOND

PRAY: Heavenly Father, thank You for giving me instructions, even when they seem strange or difficult to me.

HIGHLIGHT

OLDER KIDS: Joshua 7:1,10-12
YOUNGER KIDS: Joshua 7:1
MEMORY VERSE: Joshua 24:14

EXPLAIN

- God instructed the Israelites not to take anything for themselves from Jericho when they conquered the city.
- Achan, one of the Israelites, disobeyed God's instructions. He took some treasures from Jericho for himself. He sinned against God.
- God knew what Achan had done. He punished Achan and all of the Israelites because of Achan's sinful action.
- God told the Israelites not to take any treasures from Jericho for themselves. Achan sinned by going against God's command. Achan stole treasures and hid them in his tent. God knew about Achan's disobedience and punished him and all of the Israelites because of his sin.

APPLY

God sees everything—even our sin. God hates sin. Jesus was the only man who lived without sin, but He still took the punishment for our sin. When we ask God to forgive us for our wrongs, He does so because Jesus already paid the price for our sin. Find and circle the pile of treasures that matches the circled pile.

RESPOND

PRAY: Jesus, thank You for paying the price for my sin so I can be forgiven.

HIGHLIGHT

OLDER KIDS: Joshua 23:6-10
YOUNGER KIDS: Joshua 23:6-8
MEMORY VERSE: Joshua 24:14

EXPLAIN

- A long time passed, and Joshua grew old. He gathered all the Israelites together and spoke to them one final time before he died.
- Joshua reminded them of everything God had done for them, how God had fought for them and led them to the promised land, and that God kept His promises.
- Joshua reminded the people to obey the laws God had given to Moses. He urged them to remain faithful and to always follow God.
- The Israelites had been in the promised land for a long time, and Joshua had grown old in age. Joshua reminded the people of God's power, and how God had kept His promises to them. He also warned the people to obey the laws God gave Moses, and he told them to always follow God.

APPLY

Joshua reminded the Israelites to love God and be faithful to Him. We show our love and faithfulness to God by serving, worshiping, and obeying Him. Fill in the blanks to reveal this week's Memory Verse.

"_____ FEAR THE LORD

_____ HIM

_____ • _____ THE GODS

_____ RIVER AND

IN EGYPT _____ ."

RESPOND

PRAY: God, thank You for always keeping Your promises. Please help me to serve, worship, and obey You.

HIGHLIGHT

OLDER KIDS: Judges 3:7-11
YOUNGER KIDS: Judges 3:7-8
MEMORY VERSE: Joshua 24:14

EXPLAIN

- After Joshua died, the Israelites forgot about serving God and worshiped false gods.
- God was angry with the Israelites and let them be captured and ruled by enemies.
- The Israelites cried out to God, and He sent judges to lead the people and remind them to follow the Lord.
- The Israelites did not listen to Joshua's warning to remember God. They forgot about Him and worshiped idols. God was angry with the Israelites and let them be captured by their enemies—for 8 years! When the Israelites finally cried out to God, He sent a leader—a judge—to lead and help them follow the Lord again.

APPLY

God used the judges to save the Israelites from the consequences of their sin. But it didn't last. Only Jesus can save us from our sin forever. Follow each letter's path and write them in the circles at the end of their paths.

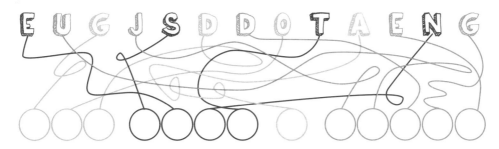

RESPOND

PRAY: Jesus, thank You for paying the price for my sin so I can be forgiven forever.

HIGHLIGHT

OLDER KIDS: Judges 4:1-5
YOUNGER KIDS: Judges 4:4-5
MEMORY VERSE: Joshua 24:14

EXPLAIN

- Once again, the Israelites forgot about serving God, so as punishment for their disobedience, God let them be conquered and ruled by a mean king for 20 years.
- Deborah was another judge for Israel.
- God used Deborah and other warriors to free the Israelites from the mean king, Jabin of Canaan.
- The Israelites continued to forget about serving God, so God allowed the people to be ruled by the king of Canaan. When the people cried out to God, He used Deborah to help free the Israelites from Canaan's king.

APPLY

God uses people to help carry out His plan. His plan is to do what is good for us and bring glory to Himself. God can use you to bring glory to Himself, too! Decode the message with the key on the right.

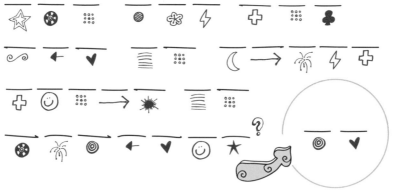

RESPOND

PRAY: Heavenly Father, thank You for using people to bring glory to Yourself. Please use me to bring glory to You.

A	✿
B	☾
C	●
D	♣
E	♥
F	★
G	✚
H	✸
I	❀
J	❀
K	◉
L	☺
M	◎
N	⚡
O	⣿
P	✰
Q	☀
R	→
S	←
T	☰
U	∿
V	◎
W	✩
X	●
Y	✹
Z	●

HIGHLIGHT

OLDER KIDS: Judges 7:19-23
YOUNGER KIDS: Judges 7:19-21
MEMORY VERSE: Psalm 19:14

EXPLAIN

- The Israelites forgot about God again, and God let them fall into the hands of their enemies, the Midianites.
- God called Gideon to be a judge and lead the Israelites to freedom.
- Gideon led the Israelites in battle, but God fought the battle for them.
- Because Israel had forgotten God, He allowed the Midianites to conquer them. Later, God called Gideon to be a judge and lead the Israelites. Gideon was doubtful at first, but the Lord instructed Gideon. He led the Israelites into battle, but God fought the battle for them.

APPLY

God asked Gideon to become a judge so he could lead the Israelites and save them from the Midianites. When God asks us to do something, we should obey and trust Him. List three ways we can obey God.

RESPOND

PRAY: God, please help me to obey and trust You every time You ask me to do something.

HIGHLIGHT

OLDER KIDS: Judges 13:24-25
YOUNGER KIDS: Judges 13:24-25
MEMORY VERSE: Psalm 19:14

EXPLAIN

- The Israelites kept doing wrong in the eyes of God. This time, He turned them over to the Philistines for 40 long years.
- The Angel of the Lord appeared to Manoah and his wife. The angel announced that they would have a special baby who would grow up to lead Israel as a judge.
- Just as God promised, Manoah's wife had a baby boy and they named him Samson.
- Manoah and his wife were sad because they didn't have any kids. One day, the Angel of the Lord appeared to them and said they would have a son. Just like God promised, Manoah's wife had a baby boy and named him Samson. God planned for Samson to be a judge for Israel when he was old enough.

 APPLY

God promised Manoah that his wife, who had not yet been able to have a child, would give birth to a son and that he would grow up to be a leader. All of these promises came true. God always keeps His promises. Who else did God promise would have a son? (*Sarah*)

 RESPOND

PRAY: Heavenly Father, thank You for always keeping Your promises.

HIGHLIGHT

OLDER KIDS: Judges 16:18-20
YOUNGER KIDS: Judges 16:19-20
MEMORY VERSE: Psalm 19:14

EXPLAIN

- Samson grew up and became extremely strong. His strength came from his long hair, which God ordered him never to cut.
- Samson fell in love with a Philistine woman named Delilah. She tricked Samson into revealing the secret of his strength, and she sold Samson's secrets to his enemies.
- The Philistines cut Samson's hair and took him prisoner, but later Samson asked God to give him strength again so he could defeat the Philistines.
- Samson became a very strong man, and God ordered him not to cut his hair. Samson disobeyed and fell in love with Delilah, who helped the Philistines cut his hair and make him weak. Samson became their prisoner, but he later asked God to give him strength again to defeat the Philistines. Samson became strong again and pushed the temple down, killing all the Philistines inside.

APPLY

When we disobey God, we should ask Him to forgive us. Even though we sin, He can still use us for His glory. Samson was super strong! Did you know that an ant can lift 5,000 times its own weight? Figure out which of  these anteaters have captured the ant in the center of the tongue maze.

RESPOND

PRAY: Heavenly Father, thank You for forgiving me and using me for Your glory.

 HIGHLIGHT

OLDER KIDS: Ruth 1:15-18,22
YOUNGER KIDS: Ruth 1:15-16, 22
MEMORY VERSE: Psalm 19:14

EXPLAIN

- Naomi lived in Moab, a land that was not her home. Her husband and sons died while they lived there.
- Naomi prepared to return to her home, and her daughter-in-law, Ruth, insisted on going with her even though Naomi told her not to go.
- Ruth left her own home and family to go with Naomi.
- Naomi and her family lived in a land that was not their home. While they lived there, Naomi's husband and sons died. After the famine ended, Naomi prepared to return to her homeland, and she told her son's widows to stay with their own families. However, Ruth would not leave Naomi, so she went to Bethlehem with Naomi.

 APPLY

Ruth loved Naomi and stayed with her. God's love for us is even stronger than Ruth's love for Naomi. He will never leave us. Help Ruth and Naomi navigate their way to Bethlehem.

 RESPOND

PRAY: Heavenly Father, thank You for always loving me with a strong love.

HIGHLIGHT

OLDER KIDS: Ruth 4:9-12
YOUNGER KIDS: Ruth 4:9-10
MEMORY VERSE: Psalm 19:14

EXPLAIN

- Ruth met Boaz while she was gathering food for Naomi and herself.
- Boaz was Naomi's family redeemer—he was supposed to help family members out of trouble and bad situations.
- Boaz redeemed Naomi and Ruth by buying Naomi's land and marrying Ruth.
- Ruth went to gather food in the fields of Boaz. Boaz was Naomi's family redeemer, which meant he was supposed to care for her. Boaz redeemed Naomi by buying the land that had belonged to Naomi's husband and sons. Boaz also married Ruth. He took care of both Naomi and Ruth.

APPLY

Boaz redeemed Naomi and Ruth by caring for them when they couldn't care for themselves. Jesus is our Redeemer. We can't take care of our own sins—Jesus took our punishment for our sins so we can be redeemed. Find all the foods in the food jumble. Which is the food Ruth gathered from Boaz's field?

RESPOND

PRAY: Jesus, thank You for being my Redeemer and taking the punishment for my sins.

HIGHLIGHT

OLDER KIDS: 1 Samuel 1:21-28
YOUNGER KIDS: 1 Samuel 1:26-28
MEMORY VERSE: 1 Samuel 16:7

EXPLAIN

- Hannah prayed to God, asking Him for a baby. God answered her prayers and blessed her with a son that she named Samuel.
- When Samuel was a little boy, Hannah took him to the priest, Eli. She dedicated Samuel to the Lord and left him with Eli.
- Samuel stayed at the tabernacle with Eli and served the Lord. Samuel would become a prophet for Israel when he was older.
- Hannah prayed that God would allow her to have a baby. God gave her a son, and she named him Samuel. When Samuel was a little boy, Hannah took him to the tabernacle and dedicated him to the Lord. Samuel stayed at the tabernacle with the priest, Eli. When Samuel was older, he became a prophet to Israel.

APPLY

Hannah didn't know God would later use Samuel as His prophet to Israel. She dedicated Samuel to God to honor Him for blessing her with a son. God is always working to carry out His plan, even when we have no idea what it is. Fill in the blanks to complete 1 Samuel 16:7.

BUT THE LORD SAID TO SAMUEL," _____

APPEARANCE _____ ,

I HAVE _____ HIM. _____

_____ OUTWARD APPEARANCE, BUT

THE LORD LOOKS _____."

RESPOND

PRAY: Heavenly Father, thank You for always carrying out Your plan.

HIGHLIGHT

OLDER KIDS: 1 Samuel 3:7-10
YOUNGER KIDS: 1 Samuel 3:10
MEMORY VERSE: 1 Samuel 16:7

EXPLAIN

- Samuel was a boy. He was living in the tabernacle with Eli, who was growing old.
- The Lord called to Samuel, and Samuel thought Eli was calling him.
- Eli taught Samuel how to respond when God spoke to him.
- Young Samuel lived in the tabernacle with the elderly priest, Eli. In these times, God rarely spoke to individuals. The Lord spoke to Samuel, though. At first, Samuel thought that the voice was Eli's. Eli taught Samuel how to respond correctly to the call of God.

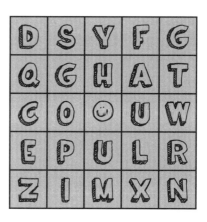

 APPLY

When God called to Samuel, Samuel replied, "Speak, for Your servant is listening." When God speaks to us, what should we do? To find the answer, begin with the smiling face in the center and write the letter for each set of directions below. Begin in the center space each time.

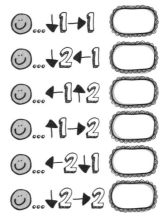

 RESPOND

PRAY: God, help me listen when You speak to me.

HIGHLIGHT

OLDER KIDS: 1 Samuel 10:17-24
YOUNGER KIDS: 1 Samuel 10:17-19
MEMORY VERSE: 1 Samuel 16:7

EXPLAIN

- The Israelites wanted a king because the nations around them all had a king.
- God told Samuel He would give the Israelites a king.
- God chose Saul to be king and had Samuel anoint him. Saul was from the tribe of Benjamin.
- All of the Israelites' neighboring nations had kings, so God's people wanted one, too. God told Samuel to give the people what they wanted. God chose Saul to be the first king of the Israelites, and Samuel anointed him.

APPLY

The Israelites did not want to wait on God's timing for a perfect king—Jesus. With a parent, discuss the following questions: Have you ever tried to do something before it was time? What happens if you take a cake out of the oven before it's done? Or try to take a bite of food before it cools off?

RESPOND

PRAY: God, please help me to wait on Your perfect timing for my life.

 HIGHLIGHT

OLDER KIDS: 1 Samuel 13:13-14
YOUNGER KIDS: 1 Samuel 13:14
MEMORY VERSE: 1 Samuel 16:7

 EXPLAIN

- When Samuel was late, Saul became impatient and disobeyed God.
- Samuel told Saul that because Saul did not wait to burn the offering, his reign as king would not last.
- Samuel told Saul that God would anoint someone else as king of Israel.
- Samuel was running late, and Saul's troops were becoming scared of the Philistines, who they thought might attack them. Saul grew impatient and didn't wait for Samuel like he was supposed to. Instead, Saul offered the burnt offering to God without Samuel. Because of Saul's disobedience, Samuel told him that his reign as king would not last. God would anoint someone else.

APPLY

Saul sinned by disobeying God. God commands us to obey Him, but we all sin and need a Savior. God sent Jesus to be our Savior and King forever. Write this week's memory verse in the circle.

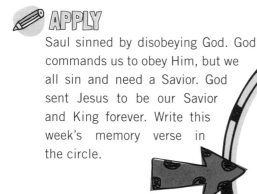

 RESPOND

PRAY: Heavenly Father, thank You for sending Jesus to be our Savior and King.

 **HIGHLIGHT**

OLDER KIDS: 1 Samuel 16:5-7,11-13
YOUNGER KIDS: 1 Samuel 16:11-13
MEMORY VERSE: 1 Samuel 16:7

 EXPLAIN

- God rejected Saul as king of Israel, so He sent Samuel to Bethlehem to anoint Israel's next king.
- Samuel thought that the new king would be one of Jesse's older sons, but God said it wasn't.
- God had chosen David, Jesse's youngest son, to be the next king of Israel.
- After Saul's disobedience, God called Samuel to anoint the future king of Israel. God sent Samuel to Jesse's family in Bethlehem. Samuel assumed that the new king would be one of Jesse's older sons, but God wanted David, Jesse's youngest son, to be king.

 APPLY

Man tends to look at a person from the outside, but God does not only look at the outside of us—He looks at our heart. In the boxes, list three things about yourself that God can see and others can't.

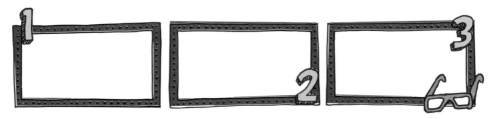

 **RESPOND**

PRAY: Heavenly Father, thank You for looking at my heart.

HIGHLIGHT
OLDER KIDS: 1 Samuel 17:48-51
YOUNGER KIDS: 1 Samuel 17:48-50
MEMORY VERSE: 2 Timothy 4:17a

EXPLAIN

- David was delivering food to his brothers, who were about to fight the Philistines.
- Goliath, a very strong and tall Philistine warrior, challenged the Israelites every day, but no one would fight him because he was too tough.
- David fought Goliath, using only a sling and stones, and killed him.
- The warrior Goliath challenged the Israelites every day, but no one would fight him. David, who was still a boy, defeated Goliath with a sling and stones.

APPLY

God gives us strength to follow His plan. Look at the chart to figure out how tall Goliath was.

RESPOND

PRAY: Heavenly Father, thank You for giving me the strength to follow Your plan.

HIGHLIGHT

OLDER KIDS: 1 Samuel 19:1-3
YOUNGER KIDS: 1 Samuel 19:1-2
MEMORY VERSE: 2 Timothy 4:17a

EXPLAIN

- King Saul was jealous and afraid of David, and Saul wanted to kill him.
- Saul's son, Jonathan, was David's best friend and loved him very much.
- Jonathan helped David escape from Saul.
- King Saul felt threatened by David, whom God had chosen to be the king of Israel, so Saul ordered his son Jonathan and all his servants to kill David. Jonathan was David's best friend, and he did not want him to be killed. Jonathan loved David very much and helped hide him from Saul.

APPLY

Jonathan was a true friend to David, just like Jesus is our true friend. He paid the price for our sins on the cross and talks to God about us. With a parent, talk about your own friendships and what it means to have or be a true friend. Do you have a friend like Jonathan?

RESPOND

PRAY: Jesus, thank You for being my friend.

HIGHLIGHT

OLDER KIDS: 1 Samuel 22:1-2
YOUNGER KIDS: 1 Samuel 22:1-2
MEMORY VERSE: 2 Timothy 4:17a

EXPLAIN

- Saul was becoming more and more jealous of David.
- David chose to run away from Saul and hide in a cave.
- David's family fled with him. In addition to David's family, over 400 other people followed David into the caves, and he became their leader.
- David fled from Saul, who wanted to remain as the king of Israel. Saul's jealousy and rage against David was increasing. David decided to run away from Saul and live in a cave with his family and hundreds of other people who followed him as a leader.

APPLY

David did not want to fight against Saul. God watched over David, even when he had to hide from his enemy. Draw David hiding in the cave below.

RESPOND

PRAY: Heavenly Father, thank You for always watching over me.

 HIGHLIGHT

OLDER KIDS: Psalm 22:27-28
YOUNGER KIDS: Psalm 22:27-28
MEMORY VERSE: 2 Timothy 4:17a

EXPLAIN

- David wrote this psalm while he was running from Saul.
- David called on God directly to deliver him from his cruel enemies.
- David understood that God was still in control. He wrote that, eventually, all people would come to realize the Lord's enduring power.
- Even though David was running for his life and surrounded by people who wanted to hurt him, he knew that even in the middle of trouble, God is still our King.

 APPLY

Even when hard things happen, God is still in control. Use the music scale key to fill in the missing letters in the phrases below.

__O__ IS __LW__YS IN __ONTROL

__V__N __URING H__RD TIM__S.

 **RESPOND**

PRAY: God, thank You for always being in control.

HIGHLIGHT

OLDER KIDS: 1 Samuel 28:15-19
YOUNGER KIDS: 1 Samuel 28:15-17
MEMORY VERSE: 2 Timothy 4:17a

EXPLAIN

- God had rejected Saul because Saul had disobeyed Him for so long.
- Samuel told Saul that God would do exactly as He said before.
- Samuel told Saul that he and his sons would die the next day and that the Philistines would conquer Israel.
- God was angry with Saul and rejected him as king of Israel because of his disobedience. Saul called on Samuel for advice. Samuel reminded Saul of his sins against the Lord, saying that God would do exactly what He had warned Saul He would do, and that He would make David king of Israel. Samuel also told Saul that he would die in battle the next day against the Philistines.

APPLY

God hates sin and cannot be near it. Because Jesus paid the price for our sins, we can be forgiven. When we are forgiven of our sins, when will God leave us?

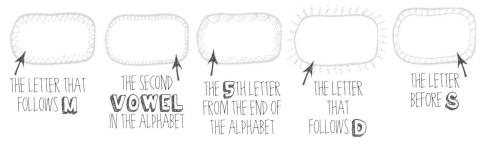

THE LETTER THAT FOLLOWS **M**

THE SECOND **VOWEL** IN THE ALPHABET

THE **5**TH LETTER FROM THE END OF THE ALPHABET

THE LETTER THAT FOLLOWS **D**

THE LETTER BEFORE **S**

RESPOND

PRAY: Jesus, thank You for paying the price for my sins so I can be with God forever.

HIGHLIGHT

OLDER KIDS: 2 Samuel 2:5-7
YOUNGER KIDS: 2 Samuel 2:5-7
MEMORY VERSE: Psalm 51:10

EXPLAIN

- David became king after Saul died.
- David honored the men who were kind to Saul's family.
- David respected Saul even when Saul was unkind to him, because David knew God had made Saul king.
- Saul died and David became king. Even though Saul had tried to kill David, David honored the men who were kind to Saul's family after he died.

 APPLY

It honors God when we are kind to others, even if they are not kind to us. List three ways you can be kind to others.

 **RESPOND**

PRAY: God, help me honor You by being kind to others.

HIGHLIGHT

OLDER KIDS: Psalm 23
YOUNGER KIDS: Psalm 23:1-3
MEMORY VERSE: Psalm 51:10

EXPLAIN

- God cares for us like a shepherd cares for his sheep.
- God is a kind and strong shepherd.
- We have everything we need because God cares for us.
- God is like a good shepherd, and we are like His sheep. God protects us and cares for us like a shepherd takes care of his sheep. We have everything we need because God takes care of us. God protects us from enemies.

APPLY

We can trust God to protect and take care of us. Find your way through the maze to reach the sheep.

RESPOND

PRAY: Heavenly Father, thank You for caring for me and taking care of me.

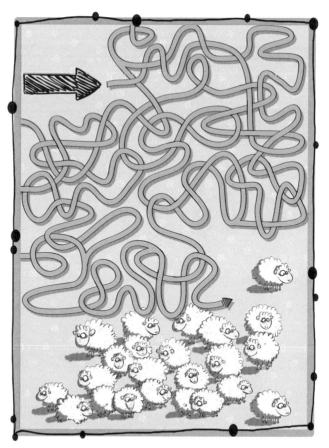

HIGHLIGHT

OLDER KIDS: 2 Samuel 7:8-11
YOUNGER KIDS: 2 Samuel 7:8-9
MEMORY VERSE: Psalm 51:10

EXPLAIN

- God made a covenant (special promise) with David.
- God promised future kings of Israel would come from David's family.
- God promised David's kingdom would last forever.
- After David became king, God made a covenant with him. God told David that future kings of Israel would come from his family and that David's kingdom would last forever.

 APPLY

God kept His promise by sending Jesus as one of David's descendants. Fill in each square by writing the first letter of each object to find out how long Jesus' kingdom will last.

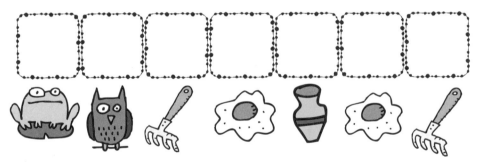

RESPOND

PRAY: God, thank You for sending Jesus to be our King forever.

HIGHLIGHT

OLDER KIDS: 2 Samuel 9:3-7
YOUNGER KIDS: 2 Samuel 9:6-7
MEMORY VERSE: Psalm 51:10

EXPLAIN

- David showed grace and kindness to Saul's family.
- David gave Jonathan's son, Mephibosheth, the things that had belonged to his grandfather, Saul.
- David honored Mephibosheth because of his grandfather, Saul.
- Even though Saul had become David's enemy, David wanted to show grace (kindness they did not deserve) to Saul's family. David gave Jonathan's son the things that had belonged to his grandfather, Saul. David honored Mephibosheth because of Saul.

APPLY

David gave grace to Mephibosheth when he did nothing to deserve it. God gives grace to us when we do not deserve it. With a parent, discuss what it means to show grace. Has someone ever done something nice for you when you didn't deserve it?

RESPOND

PRAY: Heavenly Father, thank You for giving me grace even though I don't deserve it.

HIGHLIGHT

OLDER KIDS: 2 Samuel 12:7-10
YOUNGER KIDS: 2 Samuel 12:7-9
MEMORY VERSE: Psalm 51:10

EXPLAIN

- David had sinned against God. David sinned and even had a person killed to help cover up his sin.
- The prophet Nathan used a parable, or story, to explain to David how he sinned.
- God punished David for his sin, but God also forgave David.
- David chose to disobey God. Using a story, the prophet Nathan explained to David that he had done wrong to a good man. David understood his sin and was sorry. God forgave David, but David still had to suffer for his sin.

 APPLY

Jesus paid the full punishment for our sin so we can be forgiven. Use the jumbled words to help you recall Psalm 51:10, then write the verse.

 RESPOND

PRAY: Jesus, thank You for paying the ultimate price for my sin so I can be forgiven.

SPIRIT ME CLEAN CREATE HEART GOD RENEW

HIGHLIGHT

OLDER KIDS: Psalm 51:1-5
YOUNGER KIDS: Psalm 51:2-4
MEMORY VERSE: Psalm 119:11

EXPLAIN

- David wrote this psalm after Nathan talked to him about his sin.
- David recognized his bad actions and was sorry. He confessed, or admitted, his sin and asked God to forgive him.
- David praised God, even though he was ashamed. David understood that God is perfect. God cannot have sin in His presence. David asked for God's forgiveness.
- After the prophet Nathan talked to him about his choice to sin against God, David wrote Psalm 51. David realized his sin, and he confessed, or admitted, his sin. David asked God to forgive him. David understood why the Lord had to punish him since God is blameless and perfect.

APPLY

Just like David in today's passage, we need to confess our sin and ask God to forgive us when we disobey Him. Discuss the following questions with a parent: Have you ever asked anyone to forgive you? Have you ever forgiven anyone?

RESPOND

PRAY: Heavenly Father, thank You for forgiving me when I ask You for forgiveness.

HIGHLIGHT

OLDER KIDS: Psalm 24:7-10
YOUNGER KIDS: Psalm 24:7-10
MEMORY VERSE: Psalm 119:11

EXPLAIN

- Psalm 24 was also written by David.
- David began this psalm by writing about God's creation.
- God owns everything in creation. God is the King of glory.
- In this psalm, David meditated on the Creator God—He is in control of the earth and everything on it. David urged us to remember God's power and told us we should seek God, King of everything.

APPLY

Jesus gives us clean hands and hearts, and He helps us set our minds on what is true so we can worship God. Find the hand and heart that don't match the others.

RESPOND

PRAY: Jesus, thank You for helping me focus on what is true so I can worship God.

HIGHLIGHT

OLDER KIDS: Psalm 1:1-3
YOUNGER KIDS: Psalm 1:1-2
MEMORY VERSE: Psalm 119:11

EXPLAIN

- In this psalm, David reminds us we will be joyful when we follow God's instructions.
- Instead of paying attention to the advice of sinful people, we should listen to God and His commands.
- We should think about God's commands every day and night.
- We have a choice. We can listen to the Lord and those who speak His truth, or we can listen to sinful voices. Only one of those choices leads to happiness. When we follow God's instructions, we will be joyful, but doing wicked things leads us to trouble.

APPLY

Our joy comes from obeying God's commands. Color in the words from the memory verse (Psalm 119:11), then write the verse at the bottom of the page.

RESPOND

PRAY: Heavenly Father, help me to obey Your commands and find my joy in You.

HIGHLIGHT

OLDER KIDS: Psalm 119:9-11
YOUNGER KIDS: Psalm 119:9-11
MEMORY VERSE: Psalm 119:11

EXPLAIN

- David wrote that we should seek God with our whole heart.
- One of the best ways you can follow God is by knowing His Word by heart and memorizing passages.
- Knowing God's Word will also help us make good choices.
- God helps us to keep our heart pure and obey Him when we seek after Him. When we know God's Word in our heart, we can better follow Him.

APPLY

By reading and thinking about God's Word, we can understand how to obey God. Cross out the words that are *objects with arms.* Then color in every word that *follows* the words you crossed out. Read the words you've colored to find a hidden message.

THE MAN KNOWING A FUNNY SOFA GOD'S RUNNING TO THE BABY WORD BECAUSE ITS SILLY SOLDIER HELPS CHAIR US MONKEYS FOLLOW CLOSELY AFTER A TEACHER HIM.

RESPOND

PRAY: Heavenly Father, thank You for giving me Your Word as a guide to help me obey You.

 HIGHLIGHT

OLDER KIDS: Psalm 119:105-108
YOUNGER KIDS: Psalm 119:105-106
MEMORY VERSE: Psalm 119:11

EXPLAIN

- God's Word guides us like a light on a path.
- We should offer praise to God. His Word gives us life.
- In his psalms, David often talked about the dangers in his life, but he always found joy when he remembered God's Word.
- God's Word guides us along our paths like light shines in the darkness, showing us where to go in easy times and dark times. David went through many dark times, but he never stopped praising the Lord.

 APPLY

God's Word guides us. By understanding and applying it, we can follow where God leads. Answer the questions to find out "what is God's Word?"

RESPOND

PRAY: God, thank You for giving me Your Word so I can know how to follow You.

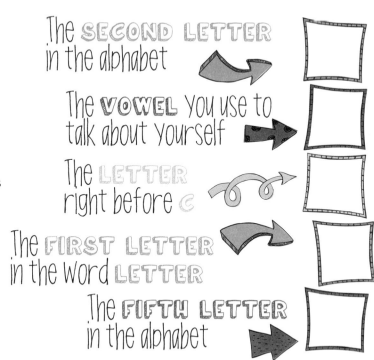

The SECOND LETTER in the alphabet

The VOWEL you use to talk about yourself

The LETTER right before c

The FIRST LETTER in the word LETTER

The FIFTH LETTER in the alphabet

HIGHLIGHT

OLDER KIDS: Psalm 139:1-3
YOUNGER KIDS: Psalm 139:1-3
MEMORY VERSES: Psalm 139:1-2

EXPLAIN

- God knows what we feel in our hearts.
- God knows everything we do and everywhere we go.
- God knows our words and actions before we say or do them. He knows everything!
- God knows what is in our hearts, everything we do, everywhere we go, and everything about us. And He still loves us! Thank God for His love!

APPLY

God knows everything about us and still loves us. Find your way to each answer in the maze. They are all correct!

RESPOND

PRAY: Heavenly Father, thank You for knowing everything about me and still loving me.

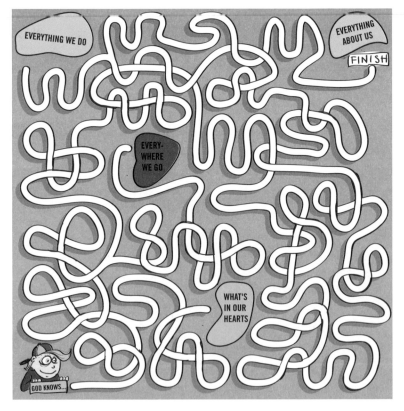

 **HIGHLIGHT**

OLDER KIDS: Psalm 150
YOUNGER KIDS: Psalm 150
MEMORY VERSES: Psalm 139:1-2

 EXPLAIN

- The final psalm in the Book of Psalms is a poem of praise.
- We should praise God for everything. We can praise Him with music and dance.
- Everything that breathes can praise God.
- This psalm, the last psalm in the Book of Psalms, instructs us to praise God every way we can. We should praise Him for all His mighty deeds and creations. Our praises can be musical or through dance, or, like David did in his psalms, through the written Word. All life that breathes will praise God.

 APPLY

Everything that breathes can praise God! List three ways you can praise God.

 **RESPOND**

PRAY: Heavenly Father, help me to praise You in everything I do.

 HIGHLIGHT

OLDER KIDS: 1 Kings 2:1-4
YOUNGER KIDS: 1 Kings 2:1-3
MEMORY VERSES: Psalm 139:1-2

EXPLAIN

- David knew he was going to die soon, so he called his son Solomon to his side.
- David told Solomon to be strong and courageous, and he reminded Solomon to always follow God's commands.
- David told Solomon about the promise God had made that someone in their family would be king of Israel.
- As David prepared to die, he gave Solomon instructions. David wanted the best for his son, Solomon. David told Solomon the most important thing he could do was to follow God's commands. He told Solomon about God's promise that someone in their family would be king of Israel.

 APPLY

The most important thing we can do is follow God's commands. With a parent, discuss what it means to follow God's commands.

 RESPOND

PRAY: Heavenly Father, thank You for reminding me to follow Your commands.

 HIGHLIGHT

OLDER KIDS: 1 Kings 3:7-12
YOUNGER KIDS: 1 Kings 7:9-12
MEMORY VERSES: Psalm 139:1-2

 EXPLAIN

- After David's death, Solomon remembered God and loved Him. He kept God's commandments and worshiped God.
- God asked Solomon what he wanted. Solomon asked God for an obedient heart and wisdom to lead God's people. God was pleased with Solomon's request.
- God gave Solomon the wisdom he asked for. God said that there would never be a man as wise as Solomon again in history.
- After the death of his father, David, Solomon kept his word and glorified God daily. God gave Solomon the chance to have anything, and Solomon asked for wisdom to lead God's people with obedience. God honored Solomon's request, announcing that nobody in history would be as wise as Solomon.

 APPLY

God is glorified when we ask Him for wisdom. Fill in the blanks to complete Psalm 139:1-2.

_____

YOU HAVE SEARCHED ME AND KNOWN ME. YOU KNOW

_____ UP,

YOU _____ .

 **RESPOND**

PRAY: Heavenly Father, please give me an obedient heart and the wisdom to follow You.

HIGHLIGHT

OLDER KIDS: 1 Kings 8:56-61
YOUNGER KIDS: 1 Kings 8:59-61
MEMORY VERSES: Psalm 139:1-2

EXPLAIN

- God's temple had been built, and now the Israelites had a permanent place to worship.
- Solomon praised God for keeping all of His promises.
- Solomon encouraged the people of Israel to always follow God's commands.
- After seven years of construction, God's temple was finally finished. The people could go there to worship God. God's presence would dwell there with them. Solomon praised God for keeping His promises and encouraged the people of Israel to follow God's commands.

APPLY

God is glorified when we worship Him and follow His commands. Connect the dots to finish the temple.

RESPOND

PRAY: God, please help me glorify You and follow Your commands.

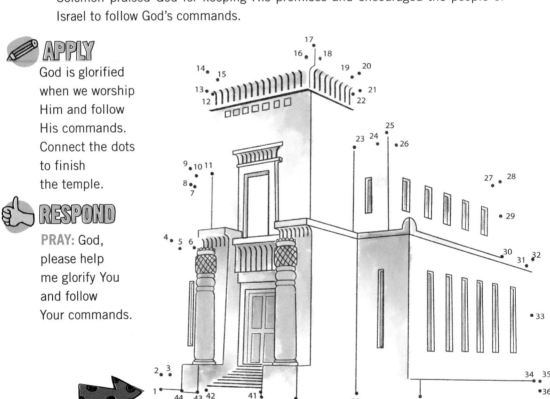

HIGHLIGHT

OLDER KIDS: Proverbs 1:1-7
YOUNGER KIDS: Proverbs 1:7
MEMORY VERSE: Proverbs 1:7

EXPLAIN

- Solomon asked for wisdom.
- God blessed Solomon with more wisdom than anyone in history.
- Solomon shared his wisdom in the Book of Proverbs.
- Solomon chose wisely by asking God for wisdom. We can learn Solomon's wisdom and discipline by studying Proverbs.

APPLY

Proverbs tells us that a wise person will listen and learn. Cross out every third letter. Then write the remaining letters in the box below to reveal an important question and answer.

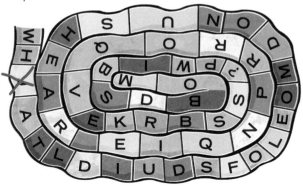

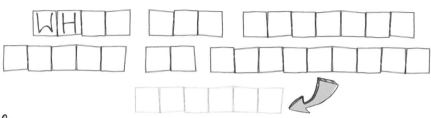

WH

RESPOND

PRAY: Heavenly Father, thank You for Your Word so we can learn and gain wisdom.

WEEK 20
DAY 2

HIGHLIGHT

OLDER KIDS: Proverbs 3:1-6
YOUNGER KIDS: Proverbs 3:5-6
MEMORY VERSE: Proverbs 1:7

EXPLAIN

- Solomon wrote lots of instructions in Proverbs, starting with keeping God's commands.
- When we obey God, it is a blessing to our entire lives.
- God will guide our lives if we follow Him and His commands.
- Solomon gave us lots of instructions in the Book of Proverbs. God wants us to keep His commands and obey Him. If we follow God and His commands, He will guide our life.

APPLY

We can't depend on our own understanding—we must depend on God. Depending on yourself won't get you very far in this maze! Follow the commands to escape from the walled courtyards: Go **north two rooms**. When you reach the room with one pink table, go **one room** to the **west**. Now turn **south** and keep going until you can't go south anymore. Go **one room** to the **west**, then **three rooms north**. This room has a small building in it. Travel **two rooms west** and then **two rooms south**. Now one **room west** and one **room south**. Travel to the **southwest corner**, then go as far **north** as you can go. Now go **one room east, one room north, one room west**. Travel **North** until you are free!

RESPOND

PRAY: Heavenly Father, thank You for guiding me and help me to depend on You.

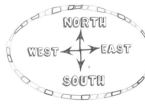

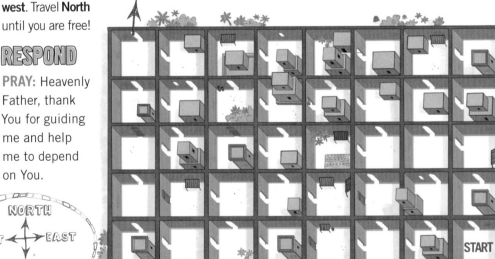

START

HIGHLIGHT

OLDER KIDS: Proverbs 16:2,18-19
YOUNGER KIDS: Proverbs 16:2,18
MEMORY VERSE: Proverbs 1:7

EXPLAIN

- God sees our hearts and knows the reasons we do things.
- If we are prideful (thinking we're super awesome all the time) or arrogant (thinking we're better than others), we will have a really hard time when we make mistakes.
- Solomon wrote that it is better to be humble and not hang out with prideful people.
- Proverbs teaches us that God examines our hearts and knows our motives (why we do things). It is much better to be humble, not prideful or arrogant.

APPLY

God's ways are better than our ways. Solve the puzzle to find a powerful truth!

RESPOND

PRAY: God, thank You for showing me Your ways in Your Word.

 HIGHLIGHT

OLDER KIDS: Proverbs 31:8-9
YOUNGER KIDS: Proverbs 31:8-9
MEMORY VERSE: Proverbs 1:7

 EXPLAIN

- Today's passage teaches that we should speak up for people who can't speak for themselves.
- We should encourage justice and defend those who are mistreated.
- We should help care for those in need.
- Proverbs tells us we should speak up for people who can't speak for themselves and help care for people who are in need. There are people all around us who are in need.

 APPLY

Everyone can help others. With a parent, talk about some ways that you have helped care for others. What are some new things you can do?

 RESPOND

PRAY: Heavenly Father, please help me to serve others, especially those in need.

HIGHLIGHT

OLDER KIDS: 1 Kings 11:9-11
YOUNGER KIDS: 1 Kings 11:9-10
MEMORY VERSE: Proverbs 1:7

EXPLAIN

- Even though Solomon was the wisest man in history, he was not perfect. He sinned against God by letting other gods be worshiped in Israel.
- God was angry with Solomon for not following Him alone.
- God told Solomon He would divide the kingdom because Solomon had disobeyed.
- Solomon was very wise, but because he was human and sinned, he chose not to follow only God by letting other gods be worshiped in Israel. God told Solomon that He would divide the kingdom because Solomon hadn't followed Him.

APPLY

Everyone sins, even Solomon—the wisest man ever. Look up Proverbs 1:7 and complete the verse on the right.

RESPOND

PRAY: God, please help me to always follow You.

THE ___ OF THE ___ ___ BEGINNING ___ ___ DESPISE WISDOM AND ___.

WEEK 21

DAY 1

 ## HIGHLIGHT

OLDER KIDS: 1 Kings 17:1-7
YOUNGER KIDS: 1 Kings 17:1-7
MEMORY VERSE: Psalm 63:1

EXPLAIN

- Elijah told King Ahab that God would not send rain to the land for a long time.
- God spoke to Elijah, telling him to hide from the evil King Ahab in a valley filled with water.
- God sent ravens to bring food to Elijah, and Elijah drank from the water hole until it dried up.
- Elijah was a mighty prophet of God who did amazing things with God's help. Elijah brought news to King Ahab of a famine that would hit the land. He told the king that God would not provide rain for a long time. God instructed Elijah to hide in a safe place that had water. While Elijah was in hiding, God sent ravens to bring food to him.

 ## APPLY

God provides for us. With a parent, talk about a time when God provided something for you or your family.

 ## RESPOND

PRAY: Heavenly Father, thank You for knowing my needs and providing for me.

HIGHLIGHT

OLDER KIDS: 1 Kings 18:36-39
YOUNGER KIDS: 1 Kings 18:36-39
MEMORY VERSE: Psalm 63:1

EXPLAIN

- Elijah wanted to prove to King Ahab that Baal was a false god, not the true God.
- The priests of Baal tried all day to get their false god to light their offering on fire, but nothing happened.
- Elijah drenched his offering in water, prayed one time, and Yahweh, God, lit Elijah's offering on fire. Then the people believed Yahweh was the one true God.
- Elijah was not afraid to stand up to the king and queen to prove that Baal was a false god. Elijah wanted to prove that Yahweh, God, was the only true God. After Elijah's prayer, and God's immediate response, the people believed Yahweh is the one true God.

APPLY

There is only one true God. Decode the message by recording the first letter of each picture in the box above it.

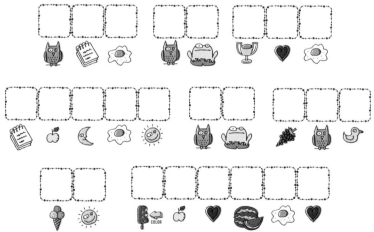

RESPOND

PRAY: Heavenly Father, thank You for being the one true God.

 **HIGHLIGHT**

OLDER KIDS: 1 Kings 21:25-29
YOUNGER KIDS: 1 Kings 21:25-29
MEMORY VERSE: Psalm 63:1

 EXPLAIN

- Ahab was an evil king who had done many terrible things.
- Elijah told Ahab that God was going to punish him for his evil actions.
- After hearing Elijah's words, Ahab repented, or was sorry, of his sin. God delayed Ahab's punishment.
- Ahab was a very evil king. Elijah told Ahab that God would punish him for his sins against the Lord. Ahab was horrified at Elijah's words and repented of the evil things he had done. No person is beyond hope or the reach of God's forgiveness.

 APPLY

God gives us grace, but there are still consequences for our sin. Sometimes someone else takes the worst of our punishment. Jesus took our consequences for sin on the cross. Connect the arrows to review each person's role from our passage.

 RESPOND

PRAY: Heavenly Father, thank You for Your grace and for sending Jesus to pay the price for my sins.

 **HIGHLIGHT**

OLDER KIDS: 2 Kings 2:11-12
YOUNGER KIDS: 2 Kings 2:11-12
MEMORY VERSE: Psalm 63:1

 EXPLAIN

- God told Elijah that he was going to be taken into heaven by a whirlwind.
- Elisha was a prophet who was learning from Elijah.
- Elisha saw God take Elijah to heaven in a chariot of fiery horses. After Elijah went to heaven, Elisha stayed behind on earth to care for God's people.
- Elijah had a successor, someone who would follow in his footsteps as a prophet of God. That man's name was Elisha. Elisha saw Elijah taken up in a chariot of fire. Elisha knew that he was to be God's messenger to the people. Elisha chose to follow God and tell the people God's words.

 APPLY

God does not leave His people without someone to help us. When Jesus left to go back to heaven, He sent the Holy Spirit to stay with us. Write Psalm 63:1 below.

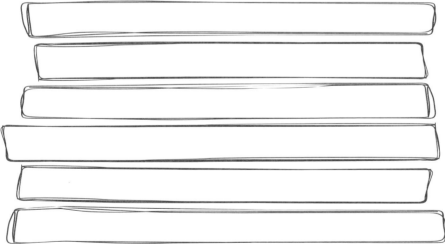

 **RESPOND**

PRAY: God, thank You for sending the Holy Spirit to be with us.

HIGHLIGHT

OLDER KIDS: 2 Kings 5:9-14
YOUNGER KIDS: 2 Kings 5:14
MEMORY VERSE: Psalm 63:1

EXPLAIN

- Naaman was a military commander who wanted to be healed from his skin disease.
- Elisha instructed Naaman to wash himself seven times in the Jordan River. Naaman didn't want to wash himself in the river, but his servants said he should.
- Naaman followed Elisha's instructions, and God healed him. Naaman believed in the one true God.
- Elisha gave Naaman instructions to wash in the Jordan River. Naaman didn't want to, perhaps because the river was dirty or he thought God might ask him to do something else. Naaman humbled himself and listened to his servant. Naaman then believed in the one true God.

APPLY

We are all sick with sin. Jesus heals us from sin when we trust Him as our Savior. Color the pictures of Naaman before and after he was healed.

RESPOND

PRAY: Jesus, thank You for being my Savior so I can be healed from sin.

HIGHLIGHT

OLDER KIDS: Jonah 1:1-4,15-17; 2:10
YOUNGER KIDS: Jonah 1:1-4, 5-17; 2:10
MEMORY VERSE: John 11:25

EXPLAIN

- God ordered Jonah to go to the city of Nineveh to preach to the people about Him, but Jonah didn't want to follow God's command.
- Jonah tried escaping by getting on a ship sailing away from Nineveh, but God sent a big storm that almost sank the ship.
- The sailors threw Jonah into the water, and God sent a big fish to swallow Jonah.
- In Jonah 1, we see the sailors praying to God because they knew God's power. They were sorry to have to throw Jonah overboard. The moment they threw Jonah overboard, the big storm stopped. God provided for Jonah by sending a big fish.

APPLY

God wants us to obey Him. Jonah disobeyed God, but God still loved Jonah. Draw on and color Jonah inside the fish.

RESPOND

PRAY: Heavenly Father, thank You for still loving me when I disobey.

HIGHLIGHT

OLDER KIDS: Jonah 3:1-5,10
YOUNGER KIDS: Jonah 3:4-5,10
MEMORY VERSE: John 11:25

EXPLAIN

- Again, God told Jonah to go to Nineveh. This time Jonah obeyed.
- Nineveh was a city full of wicked people, and God was going to destroy it in 40 days unless the people changed their evil ways. Jonah was God's messenger to them. When the people of Nineveh heard God's message, they repented of their sins and asked God to forgive them.
- God did not send disaster on the people of Nineveh because they repented.
- God had mercy on Jonah and on the people of Nineveh. God gave Jonah and the people of Nineveh a second chance. When Jonah told the people of Nineveh about God, they believed in God, repented, and asked the Lord to forgive them. God had mercy on the people of Nineveh and did not destroy them.

 APPLY

God can use our obedience to reach others and spread His Word. In the shapes below, list three ways your obedience helps others.

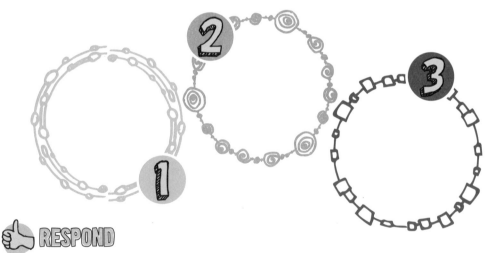

RESPOND

PRAY: God, thank You for using my obedience to help others.

 HIGHLIGHT

OLDER KIDS: Hosea 3:4-5
YOUNGER KIDS: Hosea 3:4-5
MEMORY VERSE: John 11:25

EXPLAIN

- Hosea was a prophet of God.
- The Israelites were doing evil things and not following God.
- Through Hosea, God promised He would not give up on Israel even though they would go through a long period of waiting.
- Hosea was one of God's prophets to Israel. The Israelites were practicing evil and neglecting God, choosing to worship idols and false gods instead. God used Hosea to show the Israelites how much He loves them in spite of their failure. God used Hosea's ministry to show the Israelites that He would not give up on them or forget them.

APPLY

God does not give up on us when we disobey or do not follow Him. He wants us to repent and ask for forgiveness. Use the key below to decode the message.

RESPOND

PRAY: God, thank You for not giving up on me when I disobey.

HIGHLIGHT
OLDER KIDS: Amos 1:1; 9:7-10
YOUNGER KIDS: Amos 1:1; 9:8
MEMORY VERSE: John 11:25

EXPLAIN

- Amos was a prophet of God.
- Amos warned the Israelites that God was going to punish them for the way they treated God and each other. God was going to scatter Israel from their land.
- God assured Amos that He would not completely destroy His people—His promise to Jacob was still true. God would shake the kingdom of Israel, but He would not destroy the people of Israel who worshiped Him.
- Amos was another prophet of God to Israel. God was upset at the way the Israelites were treating Him and each other. God sent Amos to warn them that their punishment was imminent—it was coming soon—and that repentance was the only way to escape destruction. Even though God said He would destroy Israel, He also said that He would keep His promise to Jacob and not destroy everyone. God planned to restore Israel to its former glory!

APPLY

When we sin, we must accept the consequences. God doesn't stop loving us when we sin, and His promises are still true. Complete John 11:25 by filling in the missing words.

RESPOND

PRAY: Heavenly Father, thank You for loving us even when we sin.

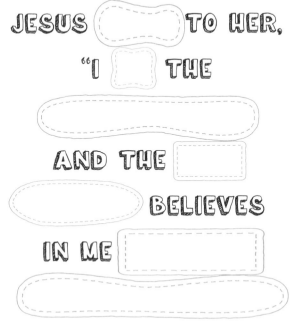

JESUS ⬭ TO HER, "I ▢ THE ⬭ AND THE ▢ ⬭ BELIEVES IN ME ▢ ⬭

HIGHLIGHT

OLDER KIDS: Joel 1:1-4
YOUNGER KIDS: Joel 1:2-3
MEMORY VERSE: John 11:25

EXPLAIN

- Joel was a prophet of God.
- Joel was sent by God to tell the people to repent.
- God sent locusts and a drought against the people of Judah to get their attention so they would listen to Him. Joel wanted the people to follow God again, or everyone would lose their harvest and their joy.
- Joel told the people God wanted them to repent and return to Him. God used locusts and drought to get their attention. Joel warned the people to repent and obey God.

APPLY

God does not give up on us when we disobey. He wants us to ask for forgiveness when we do not obey Him. Match the locusts and their words to discover the message.

RESPOND

PRAY: Heavenly Father, thank You for not giving up on me and for forgiving me when I ask.

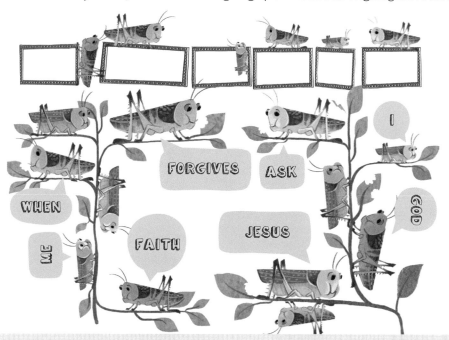

WEEK 23
DAY 1

HIGHLIGHT
OLDER KIDS: Isaiah 9:6-7
YOUNGER KIDS: Isaiah 9:6
MEMORY VERSE: Isaiah 53:6

EXPLAIN

- Isaiah was a prophet to Israel.
- God told Isaiah He would send a Messiah.
- Isaiah told Israel that the Messiah would take away the sins of the people.
- God revealed to Isaiah, one of the major prophets, that He planned to send the Messiah, whom we know to be Jesus. Jesus would do many things for the people, but the greatest would be the forgiveness of sin—a great light in the darkness.

APPLY

Long before Jesus was born, God told Isaiah that He would send a Messiah to rescue us from our sin. Unscramble these names of Jesus from today's Bible verses.

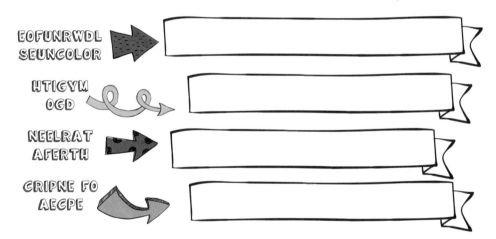

EOFUNRWDL SEUNCOLOR

HTIGYM OGD

NEELRAT AFERTH

CRIPNE FO AECPE

RESPOND

PRAY: Heavenly Father, thank You for sending Jesus to rescue me from sin.

HIGHLIGHT
OLDER KIDS: Isaiah 44:24-26
YOUNGER KIDS: Isaiah 44:24-26
MEMORY VERSE: Isaiah 53:6

EXPLAIN
- God reminded the Israelites that He alone is the Maker of all creation.
- God reminded the Israelites that He is in control of everything in the universe.
- God told the Israelites He would repair their land.
- God used Isaiah to remind the Israelites of His power. God reminded the people that He is in control and would restore their land. He kept all of His promises.

APPLY
God is in control of everything, and He has plans for His people. Beginning with the word PEDAL, follow the directions to find a new word that completes the sentence.

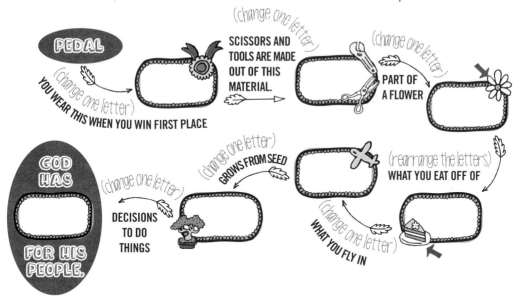

RESPOND
PRAY: God, thank You for being in control of everything and having plans for me.

WEEK 23
DAY 3

HIGHLIGHT

OLDER KIDS: Isaiah 53:6
YOUNGER KIDS: Isaiah 53:6
MEMORY VERSE: Isaiah 53:6

EXPLAIN

- Everyone sins and needs to be forgiven.
- God planned for Jesus to pay the price for our iniquities, or sins.
- God prophesied through Isaiah that Jesus would pay the ultimate price for our sins so that we could be forgiven.
- Because everyone has sinned against the Lord and needs forgiveness, God sent Jesus to conquer sin. Many years before Jesus came, God had already planned to send Him.

APPLY

Jesus died on the cross so we can be forgiven from our sin. Write Isaiah 53:6 in the box below. Use the words on the side to help you remember the verse.

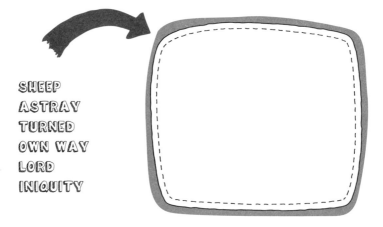

SHEEP
ASTRAY
TURNED
OWN WAY
LORD
INIQUITY

RESPOND

PRAY: Jesus, thank You for dying on the cross so I can be forgiven from my sin.

HIGHLIGHT

OLDER KIDS: Isaiah 65:17-19
YOUNGER KIDS: Isaiah 65:17-19
MEMORY VERSE: Isaiah 53:6

EXPLAIN

- In the ending chapters of the Book of Isaiah, God promised the creation of a new heaven and earth.
- In the final days, the Israelites will turn from sin, and God will respond by reminding Israel of His love. The new Jerusalem will be free of sadness and sin.
- God used the prophet Isaiah to tell Israel about God's plan for eternity.
- According to the Book of Isaiah, the people of Israel will realize their sin and ask God for forgiveness. God's response will remind Israel that He has always loved them, even though they disobeyed. He will create a new heaven and a new earth, and sin will be wiped away for all eternity.

APPLY

God has already made good plans for His people for eternity. With a parent, talk about what *eternity* means. How long is eternity? What do you think it will be like?

RESPOND

PRAY: Heavenly Father, thank You for making good plans for me.

HIGHLIGHT

OLDER KIDS: Micah 4:6-7
YOUNGER KIDS: Micah 4:6-7
MEMORY VERSE: Isaiah 53:6

EXPLAIN

- Micah was a prophet to Judah.
- Micah wrote to the people of Judah, telling them they had sinned and needed to repent.
- God promised He would send Jesus to restore Judah forever.
- Micah was a prophet to Judah, who told the people they had sinned and needed to repent. God promised He would send Jesus to restore Judah forever. God promised good things for His people.

APPLY

God will not abandon His people, even when we sin. Using the Morse Code key, decode this message.

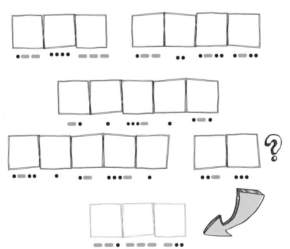

RESPOND

PRAY: Heavenly Father, thank You for never leaving me.

MORSE CODE

A	● ▬
B	▬ ● ● ●
C	▬ ● ▬ ●
D	▬ ● ●
E	●
F	● ● ▬ ●
G	▬ ▬ ●
H	● ● ● ●
I	● ●
J	● ▬ ▬ ▬
K	▬ ● ▬
L	● ▬ ● ●
M	▬ ▬
N	▬ ●
O	▬ ▬ ▬
P	● ▬ ▬ ●
Q	▬ ▬ ● ▬
R	● ▬ ●
S	● ● ●
T	▬
U	● ● ▬
V	● ● ● ▬
W	● ▬ ▬
X	▬ ● ● ▬
Y	▬ ● ▬ ▬
Z	▬ ▬ ● ●

HIGHLIGHT

OLDER KIDS: 2 Kings 17:6-11
YOUNGER KIDS: 2 Kings 17:6-7
MEMORY VERSE: Proverbs 29:18

EXPLAIN

- Time after time, Israel kept disobeying God's commands.
- God punished Israel's sin by allowing them to be captured by enemies and scattered.
- God removed His presence from Israel because of their sin and disobedience.
- Even though God sent many judges, prophets, and leaders to instruct the people how to live, Israel continually disobeyed God's commands. They adopted the sinful practices of nations God had already disowned. Finally, God allowed the Israelites to be scattered and captured by enemies, and He removed His presence from Israel. Only the tribe of Judah remained in His presence.

APPLY

Jesus paid the price for our sin so that God will never remove His presence from us. Write this week's memory verse in the box.

RESPOND

PRAY: Jesus, thank You for paying the price for my sin.

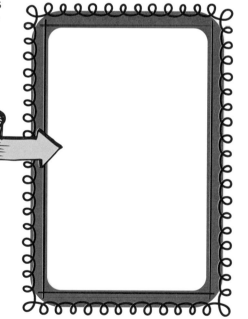

WEEK 24
DAY 2

HIGHLIGHT

OLDER KIDS: 2 Kings 19:15-19
YOUNGER KIDS: 2 Kings 19:15-19
MEMORY VERSE: Proverbs 29:18

EXPLAIN

- Hezekiah, the king of Judah, was a good king who worshiped God.
- Assyria had conquered Israel, and Hezekiah prayed for the safety of Judah.
- God did not allow the Assyrians to conquer Judah because Hezekiah was a king who honored God.
- King Hezekiah worshiped God and led the people of Judah to follow God. Assyria conquered Israel, but Hezekiah prayed for Judah's safety. God kept Judah safe from the Assyrians because Hezekiah was a king who honored God.

APPLY

God hears our prayers. In the circle write a prayer to God.

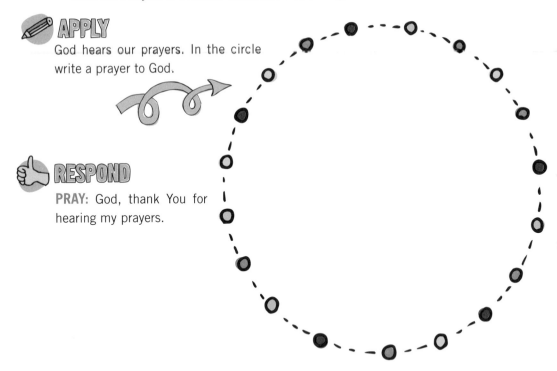

RESPOND

PRAY: God, thank You for hearing my prayers.

HIGHLIGHT

OLDER KIDS: 2 Kings 23:1-3
YOUNGER KIDS: 2 Kings 23:1-3
MEMORY VERSE: Proverbs 29:18

EXPLAIN

- Josiah became king of Judah when he was 8 years old.
- When God's temple was being repaired, the high priest found part of the Scripture and Josiah read it. He was upset because he realized the people had not followed God's laws, and God was going to punish the people.
- Josiah made a covenant to follow God in front of all the people of Judah. The people agreed to the covenant also.
- When Josiah was 8 years old, he became king of Judah. Josiah was having God's temple repaired, and they found part of the Scriptures. Josiah read it and realized the people had not been following God's laws. Josiah made a covenant in front of all the people to follow God, and the people agreed to the covenant as well.

APPLY

Josiah led his people to follow God. With a parent, discuss the need for other godly people to help lead us. Who has helped you follow God? Who can you help to follow God? How?

RESPOND

PRAY: Heavenly Father, thank You for people who help me follow You. Help me lead others to follow You.

HIGHLIGHT

OLDER KIDS: Jeremiah 1:4-8
YOUNGER KIDS: Jeremiah 1:4-5
MEMORY VERSE: Proverbs 29:18

EXPLAIN

- God called Jeremiah to be a prophet to Judah.
- Jeremiah was unsure about being a prophet.
- God promised to be with Jeremiah and tell him what to say. God had chosen him before he was born!
- God called Jeremiah to be a prophet to Judah, but Jeremiah wasn't sure he could do it. God promised He would be with Jeremiah and tell him what to say. God told Jeremiah He knew him and had chosen him before he was born.

APPLY

God knew you before you were born and has a purpose for you! Draw the words you see in each puzzle piece in its proper place in the puzzle.

RESPOND

PRAY: God, thank You for knowing me before I was born and having a purpose for me.

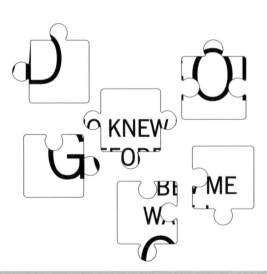

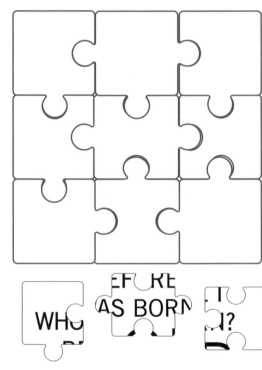

 HIGHLIGHT

OLDER KIDS: Jeremiah 29:10-14
YOUNGER KIDS: Jeremiah 29:10-14
MEMORY VERSE: Proverbs 29:18

EXPLAIN

- Even after Jeremiah warned the people of Judah not to sin, they kept sinning.
- Jeremiah told the people that God was going to allow them to be captured by their enemies.
- Jeremiah reminded the people that God would not forget them. God had plans for their future, and He would restore Judah after 70 years.
- Jeremiah warned the people of Judah not to sin, but they didn't listen. Jeremiah told the people that they were going to be conquered by their enemies. Jeremiah let the people know God would not forget them. God had plans for them, and He would restore Judah after 70 years.

APPLY

God's plans for us are good and for His glory, even when we have to go through hard times. Write T or F in each box to indicate whether each statement is true or false.

 THE PROPHET JEREMIAH TOLD THE PEOPLE OF JUDAH THAT...

⬜➡  THEY SHOULD NOT SIN.

⬜➡ GOD WOULD FORGET JUDAH.

⬜➡  GOD WOULD RESTORE JUDAH IN 70 DAYS.

⬜➡  GOD WOULD ALLOW JUDAH TO BE CAPTURED BY ENEMIES.

 RESPOND

PRAY: Heavenly Father, thank You for having good plans for me, even when I have to go through hard times.

 HIGHLIGHT

OLDER KIDS: Jeremiah 31:31-34
YOUNGER KIDS: Jeremiah 31:31
MEMORY VERSE: Ezekiel 36:26

 EXPLAIN

- God told Jeremiah He would one day make a new covenant with His people.
- God's new covenant would be different from the one He made when He led the Israelites out of Egypt. God told Jeremiah that He would place His teachings in the people's hearts.
- God said that as part of the new covenant, He would forgive sins and never remember them again.
- God declared to Jeremiah that He would one day make a new covenant with Israel and Judah. It would be a different covenant and an everlasting covenant—God would forgive the sins of all who believe. God was telling Jeremiah about His plan to send Jesus.

 APPLY

Because Jesus died on the cross for us, we can know God and be forgiven of our sin. Decode: God promised to make a new ...

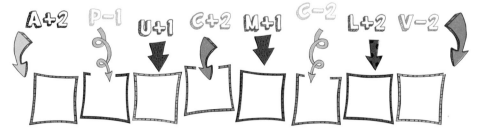

 RESPOND

PRAY: God, thank You for Your plan to send Jesus so I can know You and be forgiven forever.

HIGHLIGHT

OLDER KIDS: 2 Kings 25:8-12
YOUNGER KIDS: 2 Kings 25:8-9
MEMORY VERSE: Ezekiel 36:26

EXPLAIN

- Jeremiah had warned the people that Judah would be conquered, and it was.
- King Nebuchadnezzar's army destroyed Jerusalem, burned the Lord's temple, and tore down the city walls.
- The people of Judah were taken captive.
- Judah was conquered, just as Jeremiah had warned it would be. Judah's enemy destroyed Jerusalem, set fire to the temple, and toppled the city walls. The people of Judah were imprisoned and deported by King Nebuchadnezzar's army.

APPLY

When we disobey God, we must face consequences. Jesus took the consequences for our sin so we can be forgiven. Find the highlighted words in the puzzle below.

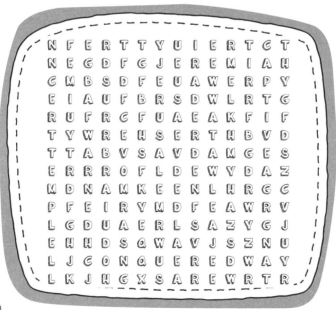

RESPOND

PRAY: Jesus, thank You for taking the consequences for my sin.

HIGHLIGHT

OLDER KIDS: Ezekiel 37:20-24
YOUNGER KIDS: Ezekiel 37:21-22
MEMORY VERSE: Ezekiel 36:26

EXPLAIN

- Ezekiel was a prophet to the people of Judah while they lived in captivity in Babylon.
- God told Ezekiel He would lead the people back to their land.
- God told Ezekiel He would restore Israel and Judah into one kingdom and He would be their God.
- Ezekiel was a prophet in the time of Judah's captivity. God used two sticks, representing Judah and Israel, as a symbol for Ezekiel to give the people. God would unify Israel and Judah into a single kingdom. As their God, He would lead His people back to their land and cleanse them.

APPLY

In a time of darkness, God used Ezekiel to share hope with the people of Judah. Today, we can share the hope of Jesus with others. Fill in the blanks to complete Ezekiel 36:26.

_____ — A NEW HEART

_____ — YOU:

HEART OF STONE

_____

HEART OF FLESH.

RESPOND

PRAY: Jesus, please help me to share Your hope with other people.

HIGHLIGHT

OLDER KIDS: Daniel 2:27-30
YOUNGER KIDS: Daniel 2:28-29
MEMORY VERSE: Ezekiel 36:26

EXPLAIN

- Daniel, a prophet who followed God, was captured and taken to live in Babylon.
- Nebuchadnezzar, king of Babylon, had a bad dream. None of Babylon's wise men could interpret the king's nightmare.
- God told Daniel what King Nebuchadnezzar's dream meant, and Daniel told the king.
- God used the prophet Daniel even as a prisoner in Babylon. Daniel followed God's laws, and God revealed the mystery of Nebuchadnezzar's dream to him. Daniel told the king his dream's true meaning, which all the Babylonian wise men had failed to do.

APPLY

Daniel trusted and obeyed God even after he had been captured and taken to Babylon. We please God when we trust and obey Him. Find your way through the maze to Babylon.

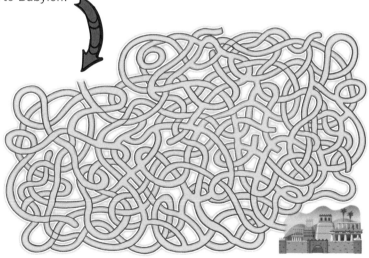

RESPOND

PRAY: Heavenly Father, please help me to trust and obey You.

OLDER KIDS: Daniel 3:24-28
YOUNGER KIDS: Daniel 3:24-28
MEMORY VERSE: Ezekiel 36:26

 EXPLAIN

- Shadrach, Meshach, and Abednego were friends of Daniel taken to Babylon.
- Shadrach, Meshach, and Abednego refused to bow down to Nebuchadnezzar's false god, so Nebuchadnezzar had them thrown into a fiery furnace.
- God was with them and protected them from harm because of their obedience. God saved them, and the king praised God.
- Even though they were in exile, Shadrach, Meshach, and Abednego remained true followers of God. Their friend Daniel's rise to a position of power had given them influence and power, too. Still, they would not worship the king's idol, so he had them thrown into a furnace so hot it killed the men who threw them in. But God kept Shadrach, Meshach, and Abednego from any harm. Seeing this, the king praised God.

 APPLY

Shadrach, Meshach, and Abednego had the courage to obey God no matter what. We can have courage to obey God even when others don't want us to. Discuss: Talk about a time you had courage to obey.

 RESPOND

PRAY: Heavenly Father, please give me the courage to obey You.

HIGHLIGHT

OLDER KIDS: Daniel 6:19-22
YOUNGER KIDS: Daniel 6:19-22
MEMORY VERSE: Daniel 9:19

EXPLAIN

- Evil men who hated Daniel tricked King Darius into signing a law forbidding prayer to God.
- Daniel prayed to God anyway, even though he knew that punishment for breaking Darius's law was death.
- Daniel was thrown into the lions' den, but God protected him by closing the mouths of the lions.
- Darius realized he had been tricked into signing the law by a group of evil leaders, but he had to obey the law even though Daniel was his friend. With sadness, he had Daniel thrown to the lions. But the lions did not hurt Daniel. God protected Daniel. The king rejoiced when Daniel was saved.

APPLY

Daniel chose to obey God, and God rescued him. Through Jesus, God rescues us from sin and death. Connect the dots.

RESPOND

PRAY: Heavenly Father, thank You for rescuing me from sin and death through Jesus.

HIGHLIGHT

OLDER KIDS: Daniel 12:8-10
YOUNGER KIDS: Daniel 12:8-10
MEMORY VERSE: Daniel 9:19

EXPLAIN

- God revealed things about the future to Daniel.
- Daniel did not understand everything God showed him.
- God told Daniel that, although many people would be saved and turn from their sin, wicked people would continue to do bad things.
- God showed Daniel pieces of the future through prophecy, but Daniel didn't understand everything God revealed to him. Not until the end of time will God's words be revealed fully; but God did tell Daniel that bad people would still do bad things, even though other people would change their ways.

APPLY

Jesus came to earth so we could be cleansed from our sin and be with Him forever. Because of Jesus' sacrifice, we have hope even when things are hard or when people do bad things. Discuss: What would you want to know about the future?

RESPOND

PRAY: Heavenly Father, thank You for giving us hope in Jesus Christ, even in hard times and in spite of other people's sin.

HIGHLIGHT

OLDER KIDS: Ezra 1:1-4
YOUNGER KIDS: Ezra 1:1-4
MEMORY VERSE: Daniel 9:19

 EXPLAIN

- Just as Jeremiah said, the Israelites were allowed to go back to Jerusalem.
- King Cyrus allowed the people to return to Jerusalem and rebuild God's temple.
- King Cyrus gave back the treasures King Nebuchadnezzar had stolen from God's temple.
- Even though King Cyrus did not believe in God, Cyrus allowed the Israelites to safely return to Jerusalem for the purpose of rebuilding God's temple. King Cyrus returned the temple treasures King Nebuchadnezzar had taken, and he even ordered his own citizens to help and support the Israelites in their safe homecoming.

 APPLY

God changed King Cyrus's heart so the Israelites could go back to Jerusalem and rebuild the temple. God can use anyone and all situations for His glory. Collect the letters in the maze to decode: Who can God use for His glory?

RESPOND

PRAY: God, please use me daily for Your glory.

HIGHLIGHT

OLDER KIDS: Ezra 3:10-13
YOUNGER KIDS: Ezra 3:10-11
MEMORY VERSE: Daniel 9:19

EXPLAIN

- The Israelites began rebuilding God's temple.
- Once the foundation was laid, the people celebrated.
- The people were thankful for God's faithful and enduring promise to bring them home.
- After being released by King Cyrus, the Israelites began rebuilding God's temple. The people celebrated as soon as the foundation was laid, singing praises and remembering God's steadfast love. God had kept His promise to bring them home to Jerusalem, and they were thankful.

APPLY

God will always be faithful in keeping His promises. Use the words around the edge of the circle to help you write Daniel 9:19.

RESPOND

PRAY: Heavenly Father, thank You for being faithful in keeping Your promises.

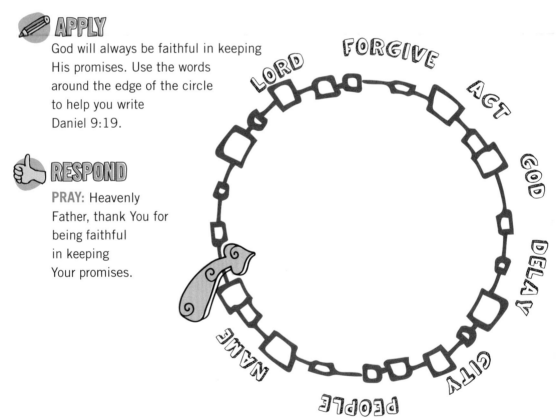

LORD · FORGIVE · ACT · GOD · DELAY · CITY · PEOPLE · NAME

 HIGHLIGHT

OLDER KIDS: Ezra 6:16-18
YOUNGER KIDS: Ezra 6:16
MEMORY VERSE: Daniel 9:19

EXPLAIN

- The Israelites had to take a ten-year break while rebuilding the temple.
- King Darius paid for the rebuilding of the temple and told the people of the land not to bother the Israelites while they rebuilt the temple.
- The temple was finally finished, and the people gathered to worship and offer sacrifices to God.
- While rebuilding the temple, the Israelites stopped the work for 10 years. God used King Darius to help the work of the temple be finished, even though he was not a believer. The Israelites dedicated God's house with joy, offering hundreds of sacrifices and worshiping the Lord.

 APPLY

God used King Darius to help the Israelites rebuild the temple so they could worship Him. God will always fulfill His promises. He can use anybody! Color all the building tools to find the hidden word.

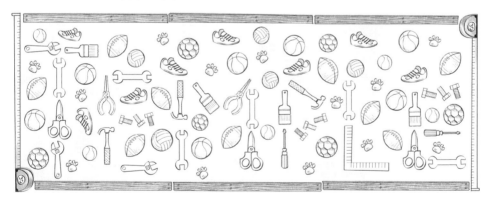

 RESPOND

PRAY: Heavenly Father, thank You for always fulfilling Your promises. Help me continue to serve You as You use me for the furthering of Your Kingdom.

 HIGHLIGHT

OLDER KIDS: Zechariah 1:1-6
YOUNGER KIDS: Zechariah 1:3
MEMORY VERSE: 1 Peter 3:15

EXPLAIN

- Zechariah was God's prophet to the Jews who returned to Jerusalem from Babylon.
- God reminded Zechariah that He had been angry with Zechariah's ancestors. God urged Zechariah to tell the people that He would return to them if they returned to Him.
- Zechariah instructed the people that God's promises are eternal.
- Zechariah, a prophet after the exile, encouraged the Israelites to love God obediently. Their ancestors had turned from God, which is why they had been punished. Zechariah reminded the people that the Lord's words, laws, and promises last forever.

 APPLY

God's promises last forever. Decode the question and answer by placing the first letter of each picture in the box above it.

RESPOND

PRAY: Heavenly Father, thank You for supplying us with eternal promises. Help me to live in Your Word and not repeat the mistakes of those who have come before me.

HIGHLIGHT

OLDER KIDS: Ezra 7:8-10
YOUNGER KIDS: Ezra 7:10
MEMORY VERSE: 1 Peter 3:15

EXPLAIN

- Ezra was a scribe (someone that wrote things down) who knew God's laws.
- The Persian king allowed Ezra to lead a group of people back to Jerusalem.
- Ezra wanted to study God's laws and teach others in Israel to follow them.
- The Babylonian king Artaxerxes gave Ezra the scribe permission to return to Jerusalem with priests, servants, and fellow Israelites. Because God's hand was on him, the king gave Ezra whatever he needed. Ezra's desire was to teach other people to follow God and His laws.

APPLY

Ezra was an example to others for how to follow God. List three ways you can show others how to love God.

RESPOND

PRAY: God, please help me show others how to follow You, leading through the example of my obedience toward You, Your laws, and Your love.

OLDER KIDS: Ezra 10:1-2
YOUNGER KIDS: Ezra 10:1-2
MEMORY VERSE: 1 Peter 3:15

- Ezra got to Jerusalem and heard about the sinful things the Israelites were doing.
- Ezra was upset because the Israelites had disobeyed God by marrying people not from Israel.
- Israel realized this sin but also realized there was still hope. A group of Israelites renewed their covenant with God.
- The people had been punished because they disobeyed. So when Ezra arrived in Jerusalem, no wonder he was upset when he found that the people had, once again, gone against the Lord's commands. But the people understood their sin, repented, and asked God to forgive them. In the presence of Ezra, they renewed their lawful covenant with God.

God has called His people to be different from people who do not believe in Him. Fill in the blanks to complete 1 Peter 3:15.

BUT _____

ALWAYS BE _____

WHO ASKS YOU _____

_____

PRAY: Heavenly Father, please help me to obey You, even though it makes me different from others.

HIGHLIGHT

OLDER KIDS: Esther 2:15-18
YOUNGER KIDS: Esther 2:17
MEMORY VERSE: 1 Peter 3:15

EXPLAIN

- Esther was a Jewish girl who had been raised by her relative, Mordecai.
- The king was looking for a new queen, and when Esther went in to see the king, she asked for very little to take with her.
- The king favored Esther over every other woman and loved her so much that he made her queen.
- Can you imagine this change for Esther? Esther went from orphan to queen. Mordecai raised her and helped her see God working in her life. God is at work in what may seem the worst of times.

APPLY

Esther suddenly went from orphan to queen. God works through situations, big and small, in unexpected ways. Complete the Esther maze.

RESPOND

PRAY: God, please work through situations in my life in unexpected ways.

WEEK 27
DAY 5

HIGHLIGHT
OLDER KIDS: Esther 4:13-17
YOUNGER KIDS: Esther 4:13-14
MEMORY VERSE: 1 Peter 3:15

EXPLAIN

- Haman wanted to have all Jews killed, so he got the king to make a law.
- Mordecai told Esther she needed to talk to the king, her husband, about the law.
- Esther agreed to talk to the king, even though she could die for going to him without an invitation.
- Haman was an evil man who worked for the king. He was acting selfishly and jealously when he got the king to make the law that would kill the Jews. Mordecai once again helped Esther see God at work in this situation. Esther was determined to face the king, even though she could be killed for approaching him uninvited.

APPLY

Esther was put in a position where her royal standing allowed her to play a role in saving her own people, but she had to take a risk. Sometimes God's plans require us to do things that require courage and bravery. Discuss: What does it mean to be *brave*?

RESPOND

PRAY: Heavenly Father, please give me courage and bravery to follow Your plan.

HIGHLIGHT

OLDER KIDS: Esther 7:1-6
YOUNGER KIDS: Esther 7:3-6
MEMORY VERSE: Deuteronomy 29:29

EXPLAIN

- Esther invited the king and Haman to a feast.
- The king told Esther he would give her anything she asked for. She asked that her people—the Jews—be saved from Haman's evil plan.
- The king honored Esther's request, and the Jews were allowed to fight against anyone who tried to kill them.
- During a banquet with Haman and the king, Esther boldly asked the king that the Jewish people be spared from destruction. The king was furious at Haman and had him put to death. Most importantly, the king honored Esther and her request.

APPLY

God used an ordinary girl to save her people. Sometimes we feel like we have to be really smart or talented or know just the right path to be used by God. But God can choose anyone to fulfill His extraordinary plans. Complete the maze.

RESPOND

PRAY:
Heavenly Father, thank You for using people like me to fulfill Your mighty plans.

HIGHLIGHT

OLDER KIDS: Esther 9:20-22
YOUNGER KIDS: Esther 9:20-22
MEMORY VERSE: Deuteronomy 29:29

 EXPLAIN

- Mordecai wrote about everything that had happened with Haman, the king, and Esther.
- Mordecai told the Jews to celebrate every year to honor how God saved them from being killed.
- God received glory for saving the Jews.
- After Esther spoke to the king, the Jews overwhelmed their enemies. Mordecai recorded the whole history and encouraged the Jews to celebrate once a year in remembrance of God's deliverance. He had used Esther to save His people from devastation.

 APPLY

The Jewish holiday of Purim celebrates and remembers God saving the Jews in the time of Esther. Discuss: How can you celebrate and remember the things God has done for you?

 RESPOND

PRAY: Heavenly Father, thank You for reminders of how You take care of us.

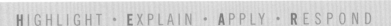

 **HIGHLIGHT**

OLDER KIDS: Nehemiah 2:1-6
YOUNGER KIDS: Nehemiah 2:4-6
MEMORY VERSE: Deuteronomy 29:29

 EXPLAIN

- Nehemiah served the king in the palace.
- Nehemiah was sad because he'd heard the walls of Jerusalem had been broken down. Nehemiah prayed to God about what he should do.
- The king allowed Nehemiah to go to Jerusalem to rebuild the wall.
- Nehemiah was the cupbearer to King Artaxerxes in the palace. Nehemiah knew that Jerusalem had been demolished, so he asked permission to help restore the city. The king listened and let Nehemiah rebuild the walls around Jerusalem.

 APPLY

Nehemiah was a servant of the king, but God called him to rebuild Jerusalem's wall. God can use anyone to fulfill His purpose for His glory. The Semaphore Flag Code is an alphabet signaling system based on the waving of a pair of handheld flags in a particular pattern. Use the flags to decode the answer: Who can God use to fulfill His purpose?

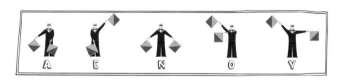

 **RESPOND**

PRAY: Heavenly Father, please use me to fulfill Your purpose for Your glory.

HIGHLIGHT

OLDER KIDS: Nehemiah 4:7-8,15-17
YOUNGER KIDS: Nehemiah 4:7-8,16-17
MEMORY VERSE: Deuteronomy 29:29

EXPLAIN

- Sanballat, Tobiah, and others wanted to stop the Jews from rebuilding the walls of Jerusalem.
- Nehemiah and the workers were not afraid. Instead, they prayed and faced the challenge.
- Half of the men worked on the wall, and the other half stood guard against the enemy.
- Enemies of the Jews did not like that Jerusalem's wall was being fixed. They planned to attack the Jews, but Nehemiah and his men remained calm and without fear. They figured out the enemy's schemes and finished the wall unharmed.

APPLY

Sometimes when we're obedient to God, others will want to stop us. God's commands are more important than what other people say. Fill in the blanks to complete Deuteronomy 29:29.

THE ( ) THINGS BELONG
TO THE LORD OUR GOD,
BUT ( )
BELONG TO US AND [ ]
FOREVER ( ) ALL THE
WORDS OF THIS LAW.

RESPOND

PRAY: Heavenly Father, please help me obey You, even when others don't want me to follow You.

HIGHLIGHT

OLDER KIDS: Nehemiah 6:15-16
YOUNGER KIDS: Nehemiah 6:15-16
MEMORY VERSE: Deuteronomy 29:29

EXPLAIN

- Nehemiah and the workers completed the wall in only 52 days.
- Nehemiah and the workers trusted God as they rebuilt the wall.
- Other nations saw God's power at work in His people.
- After only 52 days of construction, Nehemiah and his helpers finished rebuilding the wall around Jerusalem. They had put their faith in God, and God had protected them from the enemy—and the enemy was intimidated by God's great, unstoppable power!

APPLY

When God's people accomplish His work, He gets the glory. Help Nehemiah find his way to Jerusalem.

RESPOND

PRAY: God, please help me accomplish Your work and give You the glory.

WEEK 29
DAY 1

HIGHLIGHT

OLDER KIDS: Nehemiah 8:2-6
YOUNGER KIDS: Nehemiah 8:5-6
MEMORY VERSE: Nehemiah 9:6

EXPLAIN

- Jerusalem's wall had been fixed, and the people had resettled into the city.
- The people of Jerusalem devoted a day to hear Ezra read the Scripture.
- The people worshiped God, changed their hearts, and grew closer to God.
- The men, women, and kids of Jerusalem celebrated the wall's completion by gathering to hear Ezra read Scripture. Grief was put aside, and the people worshiped the Lord, celebrating their freedom from exile as they came to understand God's power as the people's support and foundation.

APPLY

Understanding God's Word makes us want to obey Him more. What's your favorite verse you've memorized? Write it:

RESPOND

PRAY: Heavenly Father, please help me to understand Your Word and obey You.

OLDER KIDS: Nehemiah 9:1-3
YOUNGER KIDS: Nehemiah 9:1-3
MEMORY VERSE: Nehemiah 9:6

 EXPLAIN

- When Ezra read God's Word to the Jews, they were reminded of the sin of their ancestors.
- They understood their need to ask God's forgiveness and to repent for their own sins.
- The Jewish people devoted more time to God's Word, then confessed and worshiped.
- After Ezra the scribe read the Scripture in celebration of Jerusalem's restored wall, the Israelites were convicted by their ancestor's guilt and failures. The people dug deeper into the Word. They praised God, remembered His majesty, and repented.

 APPLY

We must understand our sin problem. Jesus paid the consequences for our sin, though, and so God will forgive us. Follow the path to write each letter in the correct circle.

 RESPOND

PRAY: Jesus, thank You for paying the price for my sin so I can be forgiven.

 HIGHLIGHT

OLDER KIDS: Nehemiah 10:28-29
YOUNGER KIDS: Nehemiah 10:28-29
MEMORY VERSE: Nehemiah 9:6

EXPLAIN

- The Jews renewed their vow, or promise, to obey God and His laws.
- The vow included political leaders, religious leaders, and anyone who believed in God and His laws.
- According to this vow, Jews would live differently than the people who lived around them.
- The Jewish men, women, kids, and leaders recommitted their oath to God and His commands dating back to the time of Moses. Their commitment would set them apart from other people groups, but they were happy to follow God's laws together.

 APPLY

When we follow God's Word, we will be different from people who do not follow God's Word. Complete Nehemiah 9:6.

 RESPOND

PRAY: Heavenly Father, please help me to follow You, even if it makes me different from others.

YOU

YOU

HOST

THE EARTH

THEM

YOU

 **HIGHLIGHT**

OLDER KIDS: Nehemiah 11:1-2
YOUNGER KIDS: Nehemiah 11:1-2
MEMORY VERSE: Nehemiah 9:6

 EXPLAIN

- God wanted more families to move to Jerusalem.
- Not everyone wanted to move, because many already had village homes.
- The people cast lots—which was like entering a drawing for a prize—to decide who would move to Jerusalem.
- After Jerusalem's wall was finished, it was time for the Israelites to dwell in the city. But most families already owned property outside the holy city and did not want to move. To resolve this problem, the people cast lots and praised all those who moved to Jerusalem and brought glory to God.

 APPLY

God cares about where we live, and we can bring glory to God by following His commands wherever we are. Draw a picture of where you live.

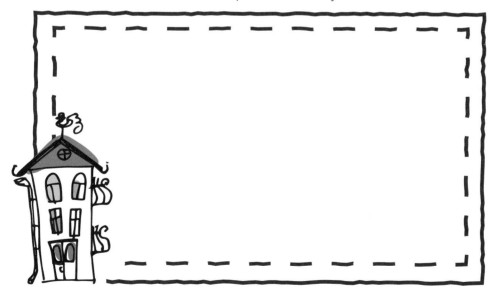

 **RESPOND**

PRAY: Heavenly Father, please help me to bring glory to You wherever I live.

HIGHLIGHT

OLDER KIDS: Nehemiah 12:27-30
YOUNGER KIDS: Nehemiah 12:27-30
MEMORY VERSE: Nehemiah 9:6

EXPLAIN

- Greater numbers of Jews were moving into Jerusalem.
- The Jews dedicated the wall with music, worship, sacrifices, and several large processions of people.
- The people of Jerusalem were so loud that their celebration could be heard from far away.
- As more people moved into Jerusalem, the holy city, they took time to dedicate the wall. The Jews recognized all that God had done and offered loud and passionate praises to Him.

APPLY

We should take time to celebrate what God has done for us as individuals and as a church. List three things God has done for you.

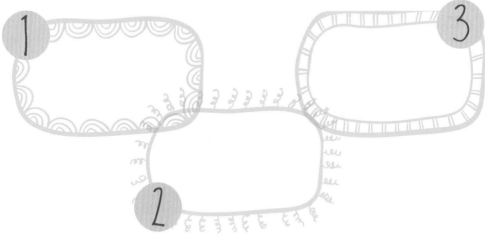

RESPOND

PRAY: Heavenly Father, thank You for everything that You have done for me!

HIGHLIGHT

OLDER KIDS: Nehemiah 13:17-18
YOUNGER KIDS: Nehemiah 13:17-18
MEMORY VERSE: Psalm 51:17

EXPLAIN

- Nehemiah left Jerusalem to serve King Artaxerxes again, as he had promised.
- When Nehemiah returned to Jerusalem, the people were not following God's laws.
- Nehemiah was disappointed and helped the people begin to follow God's laws again.
- Nehemiah had received permission from King Artaxerxes to rebuild Jerusalem's wall, but he had to return to Babylon. Nehemiah put Eliashib the priest in charge, but when Nehemiah returned to Jerusalem later on, Eliashib, the Levites, and the rest of the people had gone against God's laws. Nehemiah had to help them start fresh.

APPLY

We must always strive to follow God's laws and ask for forgiveness when we do not.

RESPOND

PRAY: Heavenly Father, please help me always to follow You.

START WITH THE WORD

SALE

REPLACE THE **S** WITH **M**

REPLACE THE **M** WITH **G**

REPLACE THE **E** WITH **S**

REPLACE THE **G** WITH **P**

REPLACE THE **L** WITH **W**

REPLACE THE **P** WITH **L**

NEHEMIAH HELPED THE PEOPLE BEGIN TO FOLLOW GOD'S

HIGHLIGHT

OLDER KIDS: Malachi 1:6-8
YOUNGER KIDS: Malachi 1:6
MEMORY VERSE: Psalm 51:17

EXPLAIN

- Malachi, the last of the Old Testament prophets, lived at the same time as Ezra and Nehemiah.
- Malachi saw that the priests were offering bad sacrifices to God.
- God is great and deserves the best and purest gifts and offerings.
- The prophet Malachi wrote against the priests' insulting offerings to God. The Creator of all deserves holy and perfect offerings. Malachi's words condemned the priests' disrespect of God.

APPLY

We should always give our best to God.
Discuss: What does it mean to give God your best?

RESPOND

PRAY: Heavenly Father, give me a heart that always seeks to give You my best.

HIGHLIGHT

OLDER KIDS: Malachi 2:10
YOUNGER KIDS: Malachi 2:10
MEMORY VERSE: Psalm 51:17

EXPLAIN

- Malachi warned the Jews that disobeying God would result in a curse.
- The Israelites were the family of God, but they were humiliating God and each other because they disobeyed Him.
- Malachi asked the people why they had turned away from God.
- Jerusalem's wall had been rebuilt, the Jews had renewed their oath and realized the sins of their past, and Nehemiah had guided them—they knew right and wrong, but they continued to shame God by sinning. The prophet Malachi asked them why.

APPLY

God calls us to live honorably for Him and to set an example for others. Who is doing the best job of following this guy's example?

RESPOND

PRAY: Heavenly Father, please help me to live honorably for You and to set an example for others.

HIGHLIGHT

OLDER KIDS: Malachi 3:7-12
YOUNGER KIDS: Malachi 3:10-12
MEMORY VERSE: Psalm 51:17

EXPLAIN

- The Israelites had fallen into a pattern of not obeying God.
- God challenged the people to give the proper offerings that God has asked them to give.
- God said if the people obeyed Him, He would bless them beyond measure.
- God spoke through the prophet Malachi, who wrote that the Israelites were robbing God. They needed to give God the offerings He called for—and if they obeyed, He would bless them so much that other nations would marvel at Israel's good fortune.

APPLY

We should give God our best, serving Him with a happy heart. Use the words below to help you write Psalm 51:17 in the box.

SACRIFICE(S)
BROKEN
SPIRIT
HEART
DESPISE

RESPOND

PRAY: Heavenly Father, please guide me to serve You with a happy heart and to give You my best.

HIGHLIGHT

OLDER KIDS: Malachi 4:4-6
YOUNGER KIDS: Malachi 4:4-6
MEMORY VERSE: Psalm 51:17

EXPLAIN

- God reminded the people that a final day of judgment would come for those who disobeyed.
- At the same time, God told the people He would provide hope for them.
- God told them a person would come like Elijah to prepare the people to be ready for His Messiah. We know now that the Messiah is Jesus.
- On the day of judgment, those with the fear of the Lord would triumph over the wicked. Malachi's final word—the final piece of advice in the Old Testament—was for the people to ready their hearts for the coming of the Messiah.

APPLY

To discover who God sent to save us from our sin, begin with the *J* in the center and follow the directions below, writing each new letter in the box.

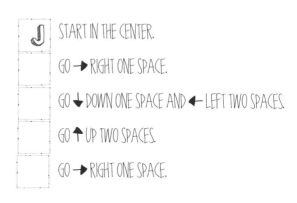

J — START IN THE CENTER.

GO → RIGHT ONE SPACE.

GO ↓ DOWN ONE SPACE AND ← LEFT TWO SPACES.

GO ↑ UP TWO SPACES.

GO → RIGHT ONE SPACE.

RESPOND

PRAY: Heavenly Father, thank You for sending Jesus so I can be saved from my sin.

WEEK 31
DAY 1

HIGHLIGHT

OLDER KIDS: Luke 1:13-17
YOUNGER KIDS: Luke 1:13-14
MEMORY VERSE: John 1:1-2

EXPLAIN

- Hundreds of years went by after God spoke to Malachi.
- An angel told Zechariah that his wife, Elizabeth, would have a baby—John.
- John would prepare people for Jesus' coming.
- People were waiting for the Messiah. God sent an angel to Zechariah. The angel brought good news! Zechariah's wife would have a baby, John, and John would prepare the way for the Messiah! John's arrival had been foretold by the prophet Malachi.

APPLY

Even after years of silence, God fulfilled the promise He had given through Malachi. Decode the question, then write the answer.

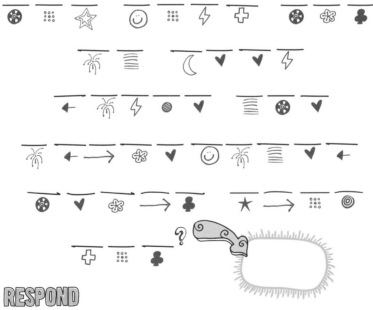

RESPOND

PRAY: Heavenly Father, thank You for always fulfilling Your promises.

HIGHLIGHT

OLDER KIDS: Luke 2:4-7,11-12
YOUNGER KIDS: Luke 2:4-7,11-12
MEMORY VERSE: John 1:1-2

EXPLAIN

- Jesus was born in Bethlehem, just as God's prophets had said He would be.
- An angel appeared before a group of shepherds. The shepherds were scared, but the angel told them not to be afraid.
- The angel told the shepherds that the Messiah, Jesus, had been born and that they would find Him lying in a manger.
- Just as God's prophets had declared, Jesus was born in Bethlehem. God told the good news to shepherds through the angel. Many angels appeared to worship God. The shepherds were excited to know about the birth of Jesus.

APPLY

God loves everyone and wants for us all to know Jesus. Color the boxes marked with a *1* blue, the boxes marked with a *2* yellow, and the boxes marked with a *3* brown to complete the city of Bethlehem.

☀ 1=BLUE
☀ 2=YELLOW
☀ 3=BROWN

RESPOND

PRAY: Heavenly Father, thank You for sending Jesus for me.

HIGHLIGHT

OLDER KIDS: Matthew 2:1-2, 9-12
YOUNGER KIDS: Matthew 2:1-2, 9-12
MEMORY VERSE: John 1:1-2

EXPLAIN

- Wise men came looking for Jesus. They had followed a star in the sky.
- King Herod was jealous of Jesus and told the wise men to report back to him about Jesus later.
- The wise men fell to their knees, worshiped Jesus, and gave Him gifts of gold, frankincense, and myrrh.
- Wise men from the east had been following a star, looking for Jesus, the King of the Jews. Herod was jealous that there was another king and told the wise men to let him know Jesus' location when they were done. The wise men did not help Herod. Instead, they praised Jesus, gave Him treasures, and avoided Herod on their way home.

APPLY

Jesus is our Savior, and He is worthy to be praised. Decode:

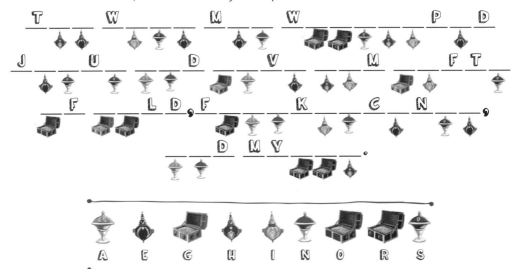

RESPOND

PRAY: Jesus, thank You for coming to earth as our Savior.

HIGHLIGHT

OLDER KIDS: Mark 1:9-11
YOUNGER KIDS: Mark 1:9-11
MEMORY VERSE: John 1:1-2

EXPLAIN

- John the Baptist was teaching and baptizing in the wilderness. He preached that someone infinitely more powerful than himself would soon come—and that someone was Jesus!
- Jesus came to John to be baptized.
- When John raised Jesus out of the Jordan River, God spoke. He was very pleased with Jesus.
- John the Baptist was preaching God's Word. People were very impressed by John's message, but John reminded them that he was only making the way for someone else, someone of incredible worth—and that someone was Jesus. John baptized Jesus, and God's Spirit came to Jesus like a dove. God was pleased with His Son.

APPLY

Jesus was baptized to show His willingness to obey God, His Father. Discuss: What is *baptism*?

RESPOND

PRAY: Jesus, thank You for being obedient to God and showing me how to obey.

 **HIGHLIGHT**

OLDER KIDS: John 1:1-5,14
YOUNGER KIDS: John 1:1-2,14
MEMORY VERSE: John 1:1-2

 **EXPLAIN**

- Jesus is called the Word. He was with God, and He is God.
- Jesus was present during the creation of the world.
- Jesus became a man and lived on earth with us.
- Jesus never sinned. He was, is, and always has been perfect. He is our eternal example of how to follow God perfectly.

 APPLY

Jesus lived on earth with us because He loves us. Fill in the missing words to write John 1:1-2.

IN THE _____ WAS THE _____,
AND THE _____ WAS WITH _____,
AND THE _____ WAS _____.
HE WAS _____ _____
_____ _____ _____.

 **RESPOND**

PRAY: Jesus, thank You for loving me and for coming to live on earth.

WEEK 32
DAY 1

 HIGHLIGHT

OLDER KIDS: Matthew 4:1,10-11
YOUNGER KIDS: Matthew 4:1,10-11
MEMORY VERSE: Matthew 6:33

 EXPLAIN

- After Jesus was baptized, He was led into the wilderness by the Holy Spirit.
- The devil tried to get Jesus to sin, or tempted Him, three times.
- Each time Jesus was tempted, Jesus used God's Word to defeat Satan.
- After He was baptized by John, Jesus went into the wilderness, where Satan tempted Him three times with hunger and power. Jesus resisted Satan's temptations using God's Word, and Jesus won!

APPLY

Jesus was the perfect sacrifice for our sin because He never sinned, even when He was tempted. Discuss: What does it mean to be tempted?

RESPOND

PRAY: Heavenly Father, please help me to follow Christ's example and not sin whenever I am tempted.

HIGHLIGHT

OLDER KIDS: Matthew 5:43-48
YOUNGER KIDS: Matthew 5:43-48
MEMORY VERSE: Matthew 6:33

EXPLAIN

- Jesus began His ministry by choosing His twelve disciples and preaching to crowds of people.
- Jesus' Sermon on the Mount taught God's people how they should live.
- Jesus commands us to love all people, even those who are our enemies.
- Jesus instructed His followers to practice loving and praying for their enemies. Jesus is a perfect example for life, and His teachings in the Sermon on the Mount show us how to have a perfect attitude and heart for God.

APPLY

God has a plan for how His people should live. List three ways you can show love to others.

RESPOND

PRAY: Heavenly Father, thank You for giving me instructions on how to act and love others.

HIGHLIGHT

OLDER KIDS: Matthew 6:9-15
YOUNGER KIDS: Matthew 6:9-15
MEMORY VERSE: Matthew 6:33

EXPLAIN

• Jesus' Sermon on the Mount continues with a command not to pray to be seen by others but to pray with a sincere heart.

• Jesus teaches us how to pray with the "model prayer," or the Lord's Prayer.

• Jesus says we should have the right reasons for doing things. We should not worry or be anxious.

• Jesus criticized the hypocrisy of people who pray to be seen. When we pray, we should pray with a pure heart or in private, and our words should be honest. We should trust God and not fear the ways of the world.

APPLY

Jesus taught us how to trust God. Unscramble the letters to decode the question. Then write the answer in the box below.

RESPOND

PRAY: Jesus, thank You for teaching me how to trust God.

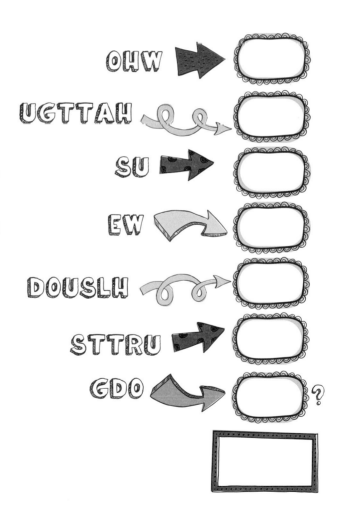

OHW ➡️ ☐

UGTTAH ➡️ ☐

SU ➡️ ☐

EW ➡️ ☐

DOUSLH ➡️ ☐

STTRU ➡️ ☐

GDO ➡️ ☐ ?

☐

HIGHLIGHT

OLDER KIDS: Matthew 7:13-14
YOUNGER KIDS: Matthew 7:13-14
MEMORY VERSE: Matthew 6:33

EXPLAIN

- Jesus continued His Sermon on the Mount. He told believers to ask, search, and knock. Jesus means that believers should pray to God about everything.
- The gate that leads to God's kingdom is a narrow one. The road that leads to eternal life is a hard one. Not many people choose to follow God.
- Jesus taught that the wide gate and easy road lead to destruction. Believers should do the right thing, even when it is difficult.
- Jesus tells us to be seekers, to ask, search, and knock continually ... and we will find. Many people will choose the easy way, but as believers we must trust in the Lord. His way is challenging, but it is worth it.

APPLY

It is not always easy to put our love and trust in God. Decode the puzzle.

RESPOND

PRAY: Heavenly Father, please help me put my trust in You, even when it is not easy.

N+ ➡

A

🐊 -ALIOR+E

AND

Replacing the final **R** with a **D**

 **HIGHLIGHT**

OLDER KIDS: Matthew 8:14-17
YOUNGER KIDS: Matthew 8:14-17
MEMORY VERSE: Matthew 6:33

 EXPLAIN

- Jesus performed many miracles. He healed a soldier's servant, Peter's mother-in-law, and many other people who were sick or possessed by demons.
- Isaiah had written that the Messiah would carry our weakness and pain.
- Jesus was the Messiah prophesied by Isaiah. He changed the lives of many and continues daily to work in our lives in miraculous ways.
- After His Sermon on the Mount, Jesus tended to people. He healed the weak, the sick, and the demon-possessed, as Isaiah had prophesied hundreds of years before. The crowds increased, and Jesus continued to teach and heal as word of His glory spread.

 APPLY

Jesus fulfilled Isaiah's words and changed many people's lives through miracles. Jesus can change you, too, by forgiving your sin and working His plan in your life. Fill in the missing words to write Matthew 6:33.

BUT SEEK FIRST

_____

AND HIS RIGHTEOUSNESS, AND ALL THESE THINGS

_____

 RESPOND

PRAY: Jesus, thank You for coming to forgive my sin. Give me a heart to let You work Your miraculous and life-changing plans in my day-to-day life.

HIGHLIGHT

OLDER KIDS: Luke 9:46-48
YOUNGER KIDS: Luke 9:46-48
MEMORY VERSE: Luke 14:27

EXPLAIN

- Jesus was with His disciples when they began arguing about which one of them was the best.
- Jesus stood a child beside Him and told His disciples that any person who welcomes a child in Jesus' name welcomes Jesus.
- To God, the least among men is considered the greatest. Jesus told His disciples to treat other people like they would treat Him.
- Jesus had just predicted His death on the cross, but the disciples did not understand His words. Then they began arguing with one another—they wanted to know which one of them was the greatest disciple. They had not understood Jesus, but Jesus understood their hearts.

 APPLY

Jesus taught His disciples—and us—that following Him is about putting other people's needs before our own needs. These girls are arguing about which one of them is the best. Can you find their matching shadow?

 RESPOND

PRAY: Jesus, please help me put the needs of others before my own.

HIGHLIGHT

OLDER KIDS: Mark 9:23–24
YOUNGER KIDS: Mark 9:23–24
MEMORY VERSE: Luke 14:27

EXPLAIN

- A father brought his son who could not speak to see Jesus.
- The father trusted Jesus to heal his son.
- Jesus healed the boy because of the father's faith.
- A man brought his son to Jesus for healing. The boy could not speak. Jesus told the man that everything is possible for the one who has faith in Him. Jesus healed the boy so God would be glorified and more people would have faith in Him.

APPLY

Following Jesus means we must _____ Him.

RESPOND

PRAY: Jesus, please help me to have faith in You.

The LETTER right before u

The LETTER right after q

The LAST VOWEL in the alphabet

The LETTER right before t

The SAME LETTER from THE FIRST BOX

WEEK 33
DAY 3

HIGHLIGHT

OLDER KIDS: Luke 12:31-34
YOUNGER KIDS: Luke 12:31-34
MEMORY VERSE: Luke 14:27

EXPLAIN

- Jesus was teaching His disciples how to live without worrying.
- Jesus called attention to the birds, the flowers, and the fields. Jesus said God takes care of these things, but He will take even better care of you, so you should have faith and not be anxious.
- Jesus instructs us to focus our hearts on heavenly treasures, not things we have on earth.
- Jesus taught His disciples not to become distracted by earthly worries and possessions. God provides for our needs, just as He provides for all of His creation. Jesus taught that we should focus on the heavenly treasure that will last forever.

APPLY

Jesus taught that the things on earth do not last forever, but the things God gives in heaven will last forever. Fill in the missing words from Luke 14:27.

RESPOND

PRAY: Heavenly Father, thank You for giving me good things in heaven that will last forever.

DOES

NOT

CROSS

AND

ME

BE

DISCIPLE.

WEEK 33
DAY 4

HIGHLIGHT

OLDER KIDS: John 4:13-15
YOUNGER KIDS: John 4:13-15
MEMORY VERSE: Luke 14:27

EXPLAIN

- Jesus spoke to a Samaritan woman who was drawing water from a well.
- He told the Samaritan woman that He could give her living water.
- The living water Jesus was talking about is the Holy Spirit.
- Jesus met a Samaritan woman at a well. Jews and Samaritans did not get along very well, but Jesus showed love toward the woman. He told her about the Holy Spirit and the Christlike faith that leads to eternal life. She recognized Jesus as the Messiah.

APPLY

When we trust in Jesus and have faith in Him, He gives us the living water of the Holy Spirit. Find your way to the center of the maze in the well.

RESPOND

PRAY: Jesus, thank You for sending the Holy Spirit.

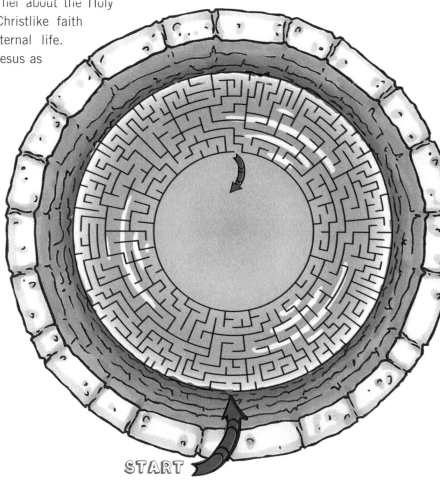

START

HIGHLIGHT

OLDER KIDS: Luke 14:12-14
YOUNGER KIDS: Luke 14:12-14
MEMORY VERSE: Luke 14:27

EXPLAIN

- One Sabbath, while Jesus was eating, He saw the dinner guests taking the best seats for themselves. In response, He taught the guests about humility, or putting others' needs ahead of your own.
- Jesus encouraged selfless behavior. He said to include poor and hurting people just as much as your friends and family.
- We will be blessed when we do kind things for people who cannot pay us back or cannot do kind things in return.
- Jesus was eating with the Pharisees. The Pharisees were watching Jesus carefully. They wanted to trick Him. Instead, Jesus taught the Pharisees, who were very concerned with themselves, how to be humble. Jesus is the best example of humility. Everything He said and did was perfect and for the good of His followers.

APPLY

God values and honors a humble attitude. Jesus humbled Himself when He came to earth to pay the price for our sin. List three kind things you can do for someone else.

RESPOND

PRAY: Heavenly Father, please help me to put the needs of others ahead of my own needs.

 HIGHLIGHT

OLDER KIDS: John 6:35
YOUNGER KIDS: John 6:35
MEMORY VERSE: Mark 10:45

 **EXPLAIN**

- A large crowd crossed the sea to find Jesus. They wanted to see a miracle.
- Jesus told the people that He is the bread of life.
- Jesus meant that He is the only one who can satisfy our spiritual hunger.
- The day after Jesus fed over 5,000 people with one small meal—5 loaves of bread and 2 fish—the people followed Him. They wanted Jesus to perform another great miracle. Jesus knew they were more interested in seeing wonderful things than understanding His eternal gift. The people wanted food, but Jesus told them that He alone can satisfy their soul.

 APPLY

Knowing Jesus is the only way to satisfy your spiritual hunger and thirst. Color all the fish that look like this:

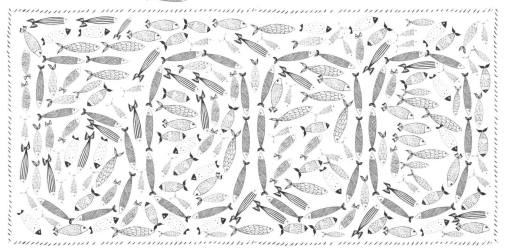

 RESPOND

PRAY: Jesus, thank You for being the only One who can satisfy my spiritual hunger and thirst.

HIGHLIGHT

OLDER KIDS: Matthew 19:23-26
YOUNGER KIDS: Matthew 19:25-26
MEMORY VERSE: Mark 10:45

MARITIME FLAGS

EXPLAIN

- Jesus said it would be easier for a camel to go through the eye of a needle (a tiny hole) than for a rich man to get into heaven.
- Jesus meant that people can't get into heaven on their own.
- With God, even something that seems impossible to people, is possible with God. God wants us to trust Him, not ourselves.
- Jesus said it would be easier for a camel to go through a tiny hole than it would be for a rich man to get into heaven. Jesus meant people can't get into heaven on their own, but it is possible with God.

APPLY

Nothing we can do will get us eternal life in heaven with God. We can only have eternal life through Jesus. Decode using the Maritime Flag Code:

RESPOND

PRAY:

Heavenly Father, thank You for providing a way for me to get to heaven and spend forever with You.

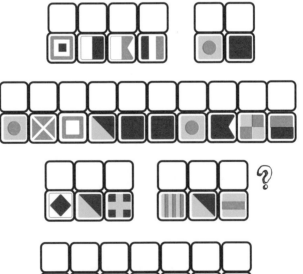

A
B
C
D
E
F
G
H
I
J
K
L
M
N
O
P
Q
R
S
T
U
V
W
X
Y
Z

HIGHLIGHT

OLDER KIDS: Luke 15:3-7
YOUNGER KIDS: Luke 15:3-7
MEMORY VERSE: Mark 10:45

EXPLAIN

- Jesus told stories called *parables* to help people understand what He was teaching.
- Jesus told a parable about a shepherd who had lost a sheep. The shepherd went looking for the sheep and celebrated when he found it.
- Jesus said all of heaven celebrates when just one person is rescued from sin.
- The Pharisees and scribes were speaking against Jesus for hanging out with sinners. Jesus told them a parable—a shepherd with 100 sheep lost one, and he left the 99 safe sheep alone to find the lost one. Jesus came to save those who were lost, just like the shepherd searched for his lost sheep. The Pharisees should have been rejoicing over a sinner who had found life in Christ!

APPLY

All people matter to God, and He is overjoyed when just one person is rescued from sin. We should celebrate too! Connect the dots.

RESPOND

PRAY: Heavenly Father, thank You for celebrating every person who loves You.

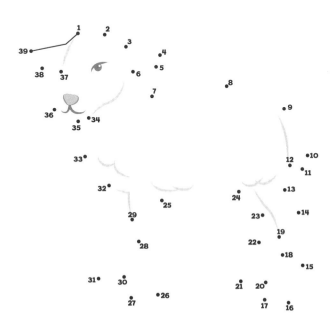

 HIGHLIGHT

OLDER KIDS: Luke 18:35-43
YOUNGER KIDS: Luke 18:40-43
MEMORY VERSE: Mark 10:45

EXPLAIN

- Jesus was walking with His disciples when a blind man called out to Him.
- Jesus asked the man what he wanted. The man asked Jesus to heal his blindness.
- Jesus healed the blind man because he had faith. The man immediately followed Jesus and praised God. So did everyone else!
- Not long before Jesus gave sight to the blind man, He had told His disciples about His death. They had not fully understood Jesus the meaning was hidden to them—but when Jesus healed the faithful blind man, the man understood.

 APPLY

Jesus has power over sickness and death. We should give glory to God for giving us a Savior in Jesus. Write Mark 10:45.

 RESPOND

PRAY: Jesus, thank You for having power over disease and death. Help me to be faithful to Your teachings and example.

HIGHLIGHT
OLDER KIDS: Mark 10:13-16
YOUNGER KIDS: Mark 10:13-16
MEMORY VERSE: Mark 10:45

 EXPLAIN
- Jesus was attracting large crowds of people who wanted to see Him.
- Some people brought young children to Jesus so He could bless them.
- Jesus' disciples got mad at the people who brought children to Jesus. They thought He was too busy to deal with kids. Jesus corrected the disciples. He invited the children close to Him!
- Jesus blessed the kids and instructed the disciples that the kingdom of heaven belongs to those with childlike faith. A person who does not come to Jesus like a child cannot inherit His gift of eternal life.

 APPLY
Faith in Jesus is not just for adults. Kids can have faith in Jesus. Write T or F in each square to identify TRUE or FALSE statements.

 People were bringing children to see Jesus, but the disciples tried to stop them.

 Jesus told the disciples He was too busy for the children.

 The disciples said the kingdom of heaven belongs to people who have faith like children.

 Faith in Jesus is only for adults.

 **RESPOND**
PRAY: Jesus, thank You for loving me. Help me to have faith in You.

 HIGHLIGHT

OLDER KIDS: John 11:17,39-44
YOUNGER KIDS: John 11:43-44
MEMORY VERSE: John 13:35

 EXPLAIN

- Lazarus was Jesus' friend. Lazarus became sick and died.
- Lazarus had been dead four days when Jesus visited Lazarus' family.
- Jesus called Lazarus to come out from his tomb, and Lazarus did. Jesus raised Lazarus from the dead.
- Lazarus's sister, Martha, told Jesus that if He'd been there, Lazarus would not have died. Jesus told Martha that He is the resurrection and the life. Martha confessed her belief that Jesus is the Messiah, who has ultimate power over life and death.

 APPLY

Jesus has total power over death. Discuss: How do you think Jesus felt when His friend died? How do you think Lazarus' family felt after Jesus raised him from the dead?

 RESPOND

PRAY: Jesus, thank You for defeating death when You died and rose from the grave. Help me always remember that You are the Messiah.

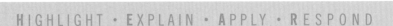

HIGHLIGHT

OLDER KIDS: John 13:34-35
YOUNGER KIDS: John 13:34-35
MEMORY VERSE: John 13:35

EXPLAIN

- Jesus and His disciples were sharing His last supper during Passover.
- Jesus gave a new command: we should love each other just as Jesus loves us.
- Jesus said people will know we are His disciples by the way we show love.
- In the final days before Jesus' crucifixion, Jesus shared a final meal with His disciples. He washed His disciples' feet and taught them that, just as Jesus— their Savior and Lord—washed their feet, so everyone should wash each other's feet. Jesus commands us to help others through love.

APPLY

Jesus shows us how to love others. We should love each other because Jesus loves us. Fill in the missing words from John 13:35.

BY THIS [   ] WILL KNOW THAT [   ] ARE MY DISCIPLES, IF YOU [   ] [   ] ANOTHER.

RESPOND

PRAY: Jesus, thank You for loving me and for showing me how to love others.

HIGHLIGHT

OLDER KIDS: John 14:5-6
YOUNGER KIDS: John 14:5-6
MEMORY VERSE: John 13:35

EXPLAIN

- After explaining His new command, Jesus told His disciples about heaven. He said He would be going away to prepare a place for them, and that the disciples would know the way.
- Thomas asked Jesus how to find heaven.
- Jesus answered Thomas that He, Jesus, is the only way to heaven.
- Jesus had already predicted His death, and now—during the Last Supper—He told His disciples that He would have to go away. Thomas grew anxious. Jesus had said that they would know the way, but Thomas didn't know where Jesus was going ... so how would he know the way? Jesus assured Thomas that He alone is the way. We must trust that Jesus is the way that we should follow.

APPLY

There is only one way to eternal life in heaven—through Jesus. Complete the maze to identify the only path to heaven.

RESPOND

PRAY: Jesus, thank You for being the way to heaven.

HIGHLIGHT

OLDER KIDS: John 16:33
YOUNGER KIDS: John 16:33
MEMORY VERSE: John 13:35

EXPLAIN

- Jesus had taught the disciples a lot of things, some of which they did not understand.
- Jesus wanted the disciples to understand and believe His teachings so they may have peace in Him.
- Jesus warned that the disciples would suffer, but they should have courage because He has already conquered the world.
- As Jesus neared His final hours before the crucifixion, He told His disciples that a day would come when He would not use figures of speech but talk about God plainly. Before that time, though, there would be challenges. Jesus assured them that He has already conquered the world, though, so they should not fear.

APPLY

When we find ourselves alone and in trouble, we can find hope and peace in the promise of a victorious Savior. Jesus has given us hope and peace because He has already conquered the world. Use the first letter of each picture to decode the puzzle.

RESPOND

PRAY: Jesus, thank You for giving me hope and peace because You have already conquered the world.

HIGHLIGHT

OLDER KIDS: Matthew 24:30-31
YOUNGER KIDS: Matthew 24:30-31
MEMORY VERSE: John 13:35

EXPLAIN

- Jesus was teaching His disciples about the second time He will come to earth.
- Jesus will come back to earth on the clouds of heaven, in power and in glory.
- Jesus will return with angels to gather His people.
- Jesus wanted His disciples to know that the world was not going to be kind to Christians. There will be wars. The sky will grow dark. And the love in many people's hearts will grow cold. Jesus promises His return, though, and He will return with power and glory.

APPLY

Jesus will come to earth again with power and glory. Draw: What do you think it will look like when Jesus comes back?

RESPOND

PRAY: Jesus, thank You for already planning to come back to earth with power and glory.

HIGHLIGHT

OLDER KIDS: Matthew 24:45-47
YOUNGER KIDS: Matthew 24:45-47
MEMORY VERSE: John 17:3

EXPLAIN

- Jesus told His disciples a parable about two servants in a household.
- In this parable, the master had gone away for a short while. One servant continued working, and the other servant stopped doing his job. The first servant was greatly rewarded. The second servant was punished.
- Jesus wants us to be faithful servants all the time because we don't know when He will come back.
- Nobody knows when Jesus will return. Jesus compared His return to the days of Noah. Before the flood, the people misbehaved, and their bad behavior continued until Noah boarded the ark. We need to stay away from darkness and live according to the promise of Jesus' return.

APPLY

Jesus will come back one day, and we should be ready when He does. Follow the paths to write the letter at the beginning of the tentacle to the flag at the end. Discover what Jesus wants us to be.

RESPOND

PRAY: Jesus, please help me to be faithful until You come again.

DAY 2

OLDER KIDS: John 17:1-5
YOUNGER KIDS: John 17:1-5
MEMORY VERSE: John 17:3

 EXPLAIN

- Jesus talked to God through prayer. He knew the time for His death was coming.
- Jesus prayed that He would bring glory to God so that He could give the gift of eternal life.
- Jesus told God that He had finished His work on earth and was ready to be glorified in the Lord's presence as He was before creation.
- When Jesus finished praying for glorification, He prayed for His disciples and for all believers. The passionate prayer of Christ should urge all of us to seek to glorify God, like Jesus, in everything we do.

 APPLY

We should strive to glorify God in everything we do. Fill in the blanks with words from this week's memory verse, John 17:3.

_____ IS ETERNAL LIFE :

_____ KNOW YOU,

THE ONLY _____ ,

AND _____

_____ .

 **RESPOND**

PRAY: Heavenly Father, give me a heart to glorify You in everything I do.

HIGHLIGHT

OLDER KIDS: Matthew 27:27-31
YOUNGER KIDS: Matthew 27:27-31
MEMORY VERSE: John 17:3

EXPLAIN

- Jesus was betrayed by Judas and arrested. Jesus was sent to the governor, Pilate.
- The people wanted Jesus to be crucified even though He had done nothing wrong. They had Pilate release a guilty criminal, Barabbas, instead of Jesus.
- Pilate's soldiers beat Jesus, made fun of Him, and placed a crown of thorns on His head.
- Jesus was betrayed by Judas, one of His own disciples. The governor, Pilate, released a violent criminal named Barabbas instead of Jesus, and the people called for Jesus to be killed. Jesus endured horrible torture at the hands of His captors, but He never complained, sinned, or asked God to stop His death. God's plan was for Jesus to sacrifice Himself so that we, as sinners, could be saved.

APPLY

Jesus did nothing wrong. He never sinned, but He took the punishment for our sin so we can be forgiven. Below is a map of Jerusalem in Jesus' day. Read the names of places Jesus visited.

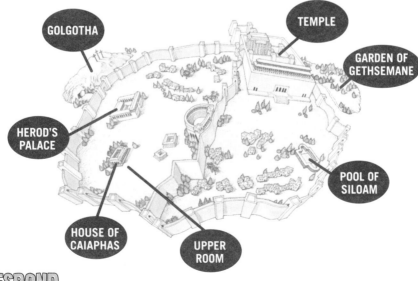

GOLGOTHA

TEMPLE

GARDEN OF GETHSEMANE

HEROD'S PALACE

POOL OF SILOAM

HOUSE OF CAIAPHAS

UPPER ROOM

RESPOND

PRAY: Jesus, thank You for taking the punishment for my sin.

HIGHLIGHT

OLDER KIDS: Luke 23:44-46
YOUNGER KIDS: Luke 23:44-46
MEMORY VERSE: John 17:3

EXPLAIN

- Jesus was on the cross between two criminals.
- The sky grew dark and the sun's light failed. Jesus gave His Spirit to God and died.
- A soldier who saw Jesus die realized Jesus really was the Son of God. The soldier started to glorify God.
- A sign saying "This is the King of the Jews" had been inscribed above Jesus on the cross. The soldiers had written this sign as a joke, but one of the soldiers watched Jesus carefully and realized that He actually was the righteous King, the Messiah. Jesus had sacrificed Himself for all who believe in Him.

APPLY

Jesus died on the cross for everyone to trust Him as Savior. Cross out every other letter to decode: Who did Jesus die on the cross for?

RESPOND

PRAY: Jesus, thank You for dying on the cross. Help me always to remember that You are righteous and the King of kings.

HIGHLIGHT

OLDER KIDS: John 19:38-42
YOUNGER KIDS: John 19:41-42
MEMORY VERSE: John 17:3

EXPLAIN

- Nicodemus and Joseph of Arimathea took care of Jesus' body after He died.
- Nicodemus and Joseph wrapped Jesus' body in cloth and used spices on His body.
- Jesus' friends laid His body in a tomb. There was a garden outside the tomb, and the tomb had never been used before.
- Nicodemus, one of the men who assisted with Jesus' burial, was a member of the Sanhedrin, the Jewish council that had plotted against Jesus. Even among Jesus' enemies, there were believers. When we find ourselves surrounded by unbelievers, we should be like Nicodemus and remember Jesus' sacrifice.

APPLY

Jesus died and was buried. Discuss: Jesus' friends loved Him and cared for Him even after His death. How do you think they felt after He died?

RESPOND

PRAY: Jesus, thank You for dying for me. Help me to remember that You died for me.

HIGHLIGHT

OLDER KIDS: Mark 16:1-8
YOUNGER KIDS: Mark 16:4-7
MEMORY VERSE: Acts 1:8

 EXPLAIN

- Three days after Jesus died, some women who knew Him went to the tomb to anoint His body with spices.
- When they got to the tomb where Jesus was buried, the stone was rolled away from the opening.
- A man told them not to be afraid—and that Jesus had risen!
- Jesus had told His followers that He would rise after three days, but they weren't sure exactly what that meant. The women ran back to tell their friends Jesus' body was gone and what the man said, but their friends didn't believe them.

 APPLY

Jesus rose from the dead just as He said He would. He conquered death and sin so we can be forgiven of our sin. Discuss: How do you think the ladies felt when the man told them Jesus had risen? How would you have felt?

RESPOND

PRAY: Jesus, thank You for paying the price for my sin so I can be forgiven.

HIGHLIGHT

OLDER KIDS: Luke 24:15-16,30-35
YOUNGER KIDS: Luke 24:15-16,31-32
MEMORY VERSE: Acts 1:8

EXPLAIN

- Two disciples were walking on the road.
- Jesus walked and talked with them, but they didn't know it was Jesus.
- When they sat down to eat, the disciples recognized Jesus. He disappeared and they ran to tell others they had seen Jesus.
- After Jesus appeared to the men on the road to Emmaus, they knew for sure they had seen Jesus. The next time they saw Him, they thought He was a ghost! But the disciples came to understand that Jesus had been raised from the dead and was alive.

APPLY

Jesus proved His resurrection so we could know He had fulfilled the Old Testament prophecies and is the true Messiah. After reading today's Scripture, complete the crossword puzzle.

RESPOND

PRAY: Jesus, thank You for being the Messiah and fulfilling the Old Testament prophecies.

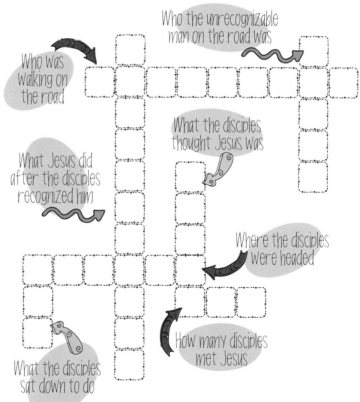

HIGHLIGHT

OLDER KIDS: John 20:24-29
YOUNGER KIDS: John 20:24-29
MEMORY VERSE: Acts 1:8

 EXPLAIN

- Thomas, one of the disciples, did not believe the other disciples had really seen Jesus.
- Jesus appeared to the disciples in a locked room.
- Thomas then believed it was really Jesus.
- Jesus made it clear there would be many people who would never see Him with their own eyes who would be blessed because they believe in Him.

 APPLY

Jesus wants us to believe in Him even if we haven't seen Him. If you were told the lines below are parallel, would you believe it without testing it? They are! Use a ruler or piece of paper to help you believe.

RESPOND

PRAY: Jesus, please help me to believe in You.

HIGHLIGHT

OLDER KIDS: Matthew 28:18-20
YOUNGER KIDS: Matthew 28:18-20
MEMORY VERSE: Acts 1:8

EXPLAIN

- Before Jesus left to go to heaven, He gave the disciples instructions.
- Jesus' instructions were for us to make disciples just like He did.
- Jesus said He will always be with us.
- The good news about Jesus and the forgiveness He gives us is for everyone! It is our job to tell people about Jesus every day as we go through our life. We should tell people about Jesus all across the world.

APPLY

Jesus wants everyone to know the good news about Him. Braille is a writing system used by people who are blind. They touch a series of bumps on paper that allows them to read, even without being able to see the words. When we tell people about Jesus, we may be able to help them see something they had been blind to! Use the braille key to solve the puzzle.

RESPOND

PRAY:
Jesus, please help me to tell others about You.

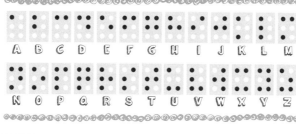

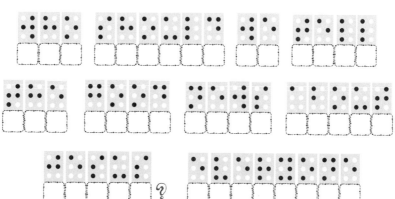

HIGHLIGHT
OLDER KIDS: Acts 1:6-11
YOUNGER KIDS: Acts 1:8
MEMORY VERSE: Acts 1:8

EXPLAIN
- Jesus was preparing to go to heaven, giving final instructions to the disciples.
- The disciples wanted to know if Jesus would restore Israel soon. Jesus said some things are only for God to know, but they should tell everyone about Him.
- Jesus went up into heaven on a cloud.
- The disciples were concerned about when Jesus would come back. He did not want them to worry about waiting around for Him—He wanted them to focus on telling others the good news about Him. Jesus will come back one day, but only God knows the day and time.

APPLY
We do not know when Jesus will return, but we should tell everyone about Him until He comes back. Fill in the missing words from Acts 1:8.

BUT YOU WILL _____ WHEN THE

HOLY SPIRIT _____ , AND YOU

_____ IN JERUSALEM,

_____ ,

AND TO THE END OF THE EARTH.

RESPOND
PRAY: Jesus, please give me courage to tell others about You.

HIGHLIGHT

OLDER KIDS: Acts 2:32-39
YOUNGER KIDS: Acts 2:36
MEMORY VERSE: Acts 2:42

EXPLAIN

- At Pentecost (a Jewish festival), Peter preached to people about Jesus.
- Peter told the people that Jesus is the Messiah they had been waiting for.
- Peter told them to repent of their sin and be baptized in the name of Jesus so they could receive the Holy Spirit.
- Jews and non-Jews (called *Gentiles*) didn't like each other very much. They each thought they were better than the other. But Peter made it clear that God's salvation and promises are for everyone, not just Jews.

APPLY

God sends the Holy Spirit for anyone who repents and believes. Decode: Who did God send the Holy Spirit for?

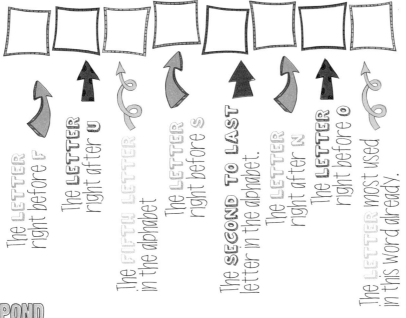

The LETTER right before F

The LETTER right after U

The FIFTH LETTER in the alphabet

The LETTER right before S

The SECOND TO LAST letter in the alphabet.

The LETTER right after N

The LETTER right before O

The LETTER most used in this word already.

RESPOND

PRAY: Heavenly Father, thank You that Your promises are for everyone.

 HIGHLIGHT

OLDER KIDS: Acts 5:12-16
YOUNGER KIDS: Acts 5:12-16
MEMORY VERSE: Acts 2:42

EXPLAIN

- The apostles (Jesus' 12 disciples) were healing people through God's power in Jesus' name.
- People would bring sick people from other towns to see the apostles.
- Many people became believers because of God's work through the apostles.
- The apostles were bringing glory to God, and sick people were being healed. People had so much faith in God to work through the apostles, they would bring sick people to the town hoping to be healed as apostles walked by.

APPLY

God has power over sickness and can work through people. Use the words provided to help you write Acts 2:42 in the box.

APOSTLES'
FELLOWSHIP
BREAKING
BREAD
PRAYERS

 **RESPOND**

PRAY: God, thank You for having power over sickness.

HIGHLIGHT

OLDER KIDS: Acts 6:1-6
YOUNGER KIDS: Acts 6:1-6
MEMORY VERSE: Acts 2:42

EXPLAIN

- More and more people became believers in Jesus.
- The disciples couldn't do the work of taking care of everyone and preach, too.
- Seven men were chosen to serve by making sure the believers were cared for.
- The number of believers had grown so much, there were too many for the disciples to take care of by themselves. It was important to choose wise believers to help. It takes a team to care for God's people.

APPLY

We can all use our abilities to serve God. Can you figure out this crazy math?

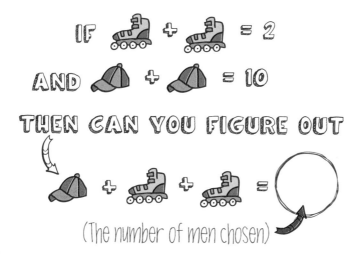

(The number of men chosen)

RESPOND

PRAY: Heavenly Father, please help me use my abilities to serve You.

HIGHLIGHT

OLDER KIDS: Acts 7:54-60
YOUNGER KIDS: Acts 7:54-60
MEMORY VERSE: Acts 2:42

EXPLAIN

- Stephen was performing signs and wonders in the name of Jesus. The Jewish leaders didn't like it.
- Stephen was taken before the Jewish court, where he preached about Jesus.
- The Jewish leaders were angry with Stephen and killed him.
- Stephen was killed for his faith in Jesus, but many people heard the good news because of his faithfulness. What people intend for harm, God can use for good.

 APPLY

Jesus told us we would be persecuted for believing in Him. Discuss: What does it mean to be *persecuted*?

 RESPOND

PRAY: Heavenly Father, please help me to be strong when I am persecuted for believing in You.

HIGHLIGHT
OLDER KIDS: Acts 9:1-9
YOUNGER KIDS: Acts 9:3-6
MEMORY VERSE: Acts 2:42

 EXPLAIN
- Saul persecuted Christians.
- As Saul was traveling, Jesus appeared to him in a bright light. Saul lost his sight for three days.
- Saul became a believer in Jesus and started preaching about Jesus.
- Saul actually wanted to kill the disciples of God. God changed Saul's heart and chose him to tell people about Him. Saul (later called Paul) traveled all over telling others about Jesus.

 APPLY
Jesus changed Saul's heart. He can change yours, too. Collect the words along the way from the outside of the maze to the heart in the center.

 RESPOND
PRAY: Jesus, thank You for having the power to change my heart.

HIGHLIGHT

OLDER KIDS: Acts 10:34-36
YOUNGER KIDS: Acts 10:34-36
MEMORY VERSE: James 2:17

 ## EXPLAIN

- Peter was speaking to the people.
- Peter understood that God doesn't have favorites—He loves everyone and wants them all to believe.
- God sent Jesus for everyone.
- Peter wanted to make it clear that the good news of Jesus is for everyone—Jews and Gentiles. Because God loves everyone equally, He wants everyone to know Him.

 ## APPLY

Who is the good news of Jesus for? Decode the puzzle to find out.

 ## RESPOND

PRAY: Heavenly Father, thank You for loving me!

HIGHLIGHT

OLDER KIDS: Acts 12:6-11
YOUNGER KIDS: Acts 12:6-11
MEMORY VERSE: James 2:17

 EXPLAIN

- King Herod had put Peter in jail and planned to kill him.
- God sent an angel to rescue Peter from prison.
- Peter's friends had gathered to pray and were shocked when he came to the door.
- God provided rescue for Peter because Peter's work for God wasn't finished yet.

 APPLY

The good news of Jesus can't be stopped by people. Discuss: How do you think Peter's friends felt when he came to the door?

 RESPOND

PRAY: Jesus, thank You that You and Your good news can't be stopped by people.

HIGHLIGHT

OLDER KIDS: Acts 13:1-3
YOUNGER KIDS: Acts 13:1-3
MEMORY VERSE: James 2:17

EXPLAIN

- The church at Antioch wanted everyone to hear the good news about Jesus.
- The church sent men out to tell others about Jesus.
- Barnabas and Saul were sent to tell others about Jesus.
- Jesus commanded us to make disciples when He gave the Great Commission. The disciples started right away. They taught others how to obey the Great Commission as well.

APPLY

We should do whatever we can to help people everywhere hear about Jesus. The church at Antioch sent men out to tell people about Jesus. You can tell people about Jesus in the places you go. As you match up the missing pieces of this town, think about all the places you go in your town that you can tell people about Jesus.

RESPOND

PRAY: Heavenly Father, please help me tell others about You.

HIGHLIGHT

OLDER KIDS: James 2:14-17
YOUNGER KIDS: James 2:14-17
MEMORY VERSE: James 2:17

 EXPLAIN

- James was Jesus' younger brother. He did not believe Jesus was the Messiah until after Jesus rose from the dead.
- James said you can't separate believing in Jesus and obeying His commands.
- James said faith leads to obedience. We can follow God's commands with the help of the Holy Spirit.
- James talked a lot about faith. He wanted us to understand that we can't follow God without also obeying Him. When we have true faith, our actions will show it too.

APPLY

It is not enough to just believe. We must also follow God's plan as God helps us. Write James 2:17 here.

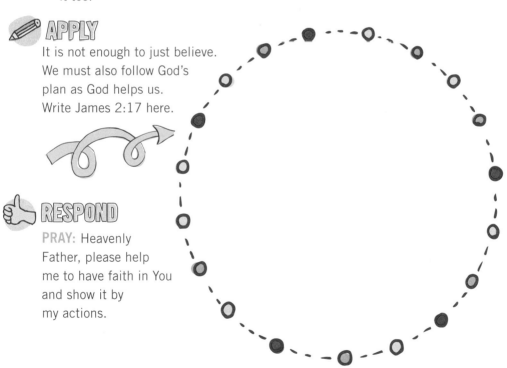

RESPOND

PRAY: Heavenly Father, please help me to have faith in You and show it by my actions.

HIGHLIGHT

OLDER KIDS: James 3:13-18
YOUNGER KIDS: James 3:13
MEMORY VERSE: James 2:17

EXPLAIN

- James was talking about how Christians should live.
- James said God's wisdom is different than men's wisdom.
- God's wisdom is pure and doesn't show favorites.
- There are two kinds of wisdom—wisdom that comes from God and wisdom that comes from people. God's wisdom is pure, but people's wisdom is not.

APPLY

God's wisdom is the best. Begin at the top of the maze and work your way down to the bottom.

RESPOND

PRAY: Heavenly Father, please give me Your wisdom.

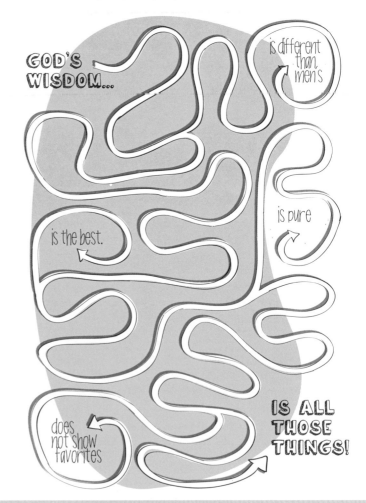

GOD'S WISDOM...

is different than men's

is pure

is the best.

does not show favorites

IS ALL THOSE THINGS!

HIGHLIGHT

OLDER KIDS: Acts 16:25-34
YOUNGER KIDS: Acts 16:29-31
MEMORY VERSE: Acts 17:24

EXPLAIN

- Paul and Silas had been put in jail but were still praising God.
- There was an earthquake, and all the prisoners could have left, but no one did.
- Because of Paul and Silas's faithfulness to God, the man in charge of the jail and his whole family became Christians.
- If the prisoners had escaped, the man in charge of the jail would have been in big trouble. Instead, the prisoners stayed where they were, and the jailer and his family became Christians. Later, when Paul and Silas were set free, they continued preaching about Jesus.

APPLY

God can use any circumstance to bring people to faith in Him. Place a check mark next to anything in this list that might bring people to faith in Jesus.

RESPOND

PRAY: Heavenly Father, please help me to have faith in You no matter my circumstances.

☑ → 🚚 Moving
☐ → 🐷 Losing all your money
☐ → 🏛 Changes in government
☐ → 🎾 Playing on a team
☐ → 🌍 Mission trip
☐ → 📖 Bible reading
☐ → 🌧 Hurricane
☐ → 🎓 Going to college
☐ → Getting lost
☐ → 💬 Having a conversation

HIGHLIGHT

OLDER KIDS: Galatians 3:27-29
YOUNGER KIDS: Galatians 3:27-29
MEMORY VERSE: Acts 17:24

EXPLAIN

- Paul wrote a letter to the believers in Galatia.
- Paul wanted them to understand there was no difference in believers in Jesus.
- Paul wanted everyone to understand that Christians are all one family—God's family.
- Paul didn't get to stay with the churches very long since he traveled a lot. He wrote letters to encourage and give instructions to the believers in the churches. He talked to them about a lot of things, but he wanted to make sure they understood God's family is one family.

APPLY

Christians are all part of the same family—God's family. Paul wanted people to understand there was no difference in believers in Christ. Can you find the shadow that has no differences from the people on the left?

RESPOND

PRAY: Heavenly Father, thank You for making all believers one big family.

HIGHLIGHT

OLDER KIDS: Galatians 5:13-14
YOUNGER KIDS: Galatians 5:13-14
MEMORY VERSE: Acts 17:24

EXPLAIN

- Paul wrote a letter to the believers in Galatia.
- Paul wanted them to understand that we are to serve each other in love.
- Christians have a responsibility to serve each other and do good to others.
- Paul made it clear that we are to love each other as much as we love ourselves.

APPLY

It is our responsibility to love and do good things for others. Fill in the missing words to complete Acts 17:24.

RESPOND

PRAY: Heavenly Father, please help me to love others as much as I love myself.

___ WHO MADE THE WORLD AND ___ IN IT— ___ LORD OF ___ AND EARTH – DOES ___ LIVE IN ___ MADE BY ___.

HIGHLIGHT

OLDER KIDS: Acts 18:9-11
YOUNGER KIDS: Acts 18:9-11
MEMORY VERSE: Acts 17:24

EXPLAIN

- Paul was traveling from place to place, teaching about Jesus.
- Some people didn't like that Paul was preaching about Jesus and tried to make things hard for him.
- God told Paul not to be afraid to keep teaching. God would be with Paul, and he would be safe.
- When people tried to make things hard for Paul or make fun of him, he could have become discouraged. But he listened to God more than he listened to people. God used Paul to spread the good news about Jesus.

APPLY

God's instructions are more important than what other people say or think about us. Decode today's application:

RESPOND

PRAY: Heavenly Father, please help me always to remember what You think about me is more important than what anyone else thinks.

A	✿
B	☾
C	◉
D	♣
E	♥
F	★
G	✚
H	✸
I	🎆
J	🍃
K	⊙
L	☺
M	◎
N	⚡
O	⁚⁚
P	✦
Q	☀
R	→
S	←
T	☰
U	∾
V	◎
W	☆
X	◉
Y	✺
Z	◉

HIGHLIGHT

OLDER KIDS: 1 Thessalonians 1:2-6
YOUNGER KIDS: 1 Thessalonians 1:2-4
MEMORY VERSE: Acts 17:24

EXPLAIN

- Paul wrote to the believers in Thessalonica.
- Paul was thankful because they had been faithful to do their best to serve God, even when they were persecuted.
- They were an example to people around them of how Christians should act.
- When we set an example, we show others how to act. Paul was thankful for the believers in Thessalonica because they had looked at his example, then set a good example for others.

APPLY

We can show others God's love by the way we act and treat others. Unscramble the words to find out some ways we can be examples to others.

athiF

opHe

unEndcrae

oveL

yJo

RESPOND

PRAY: Heavenly Father, please help me show Your love to others by the way I act.

HIGHLIGHT

OLDER KIDS: 1 Thessalonians 4:1-2,7-8
YOUNGER KIDS: 1 Thessalonians 4:1-2
MEMORY VERSE: 1 Corinthians 1:18

EXPLAIN

- Paul was still writing to the believers in Thessalonica.
- Paul encouraged them to continue pleasing God and to keep following His commands even more than they had before.
- When we reject God's ways, we reject God.
- Paul wanted the believers at Thessalonica to understand that it wasn't Paul telling the people to obey God's commands—it was *God* telling them to obey.

APPLY

We should please God and follow His commands because it glorifies Him. Decode: Who calls us to obey?

RESPOND

PRAY: Heavenly Father, please help me follow Your commands and glorify You.

HIGHLIGHT

OLDER KIDS: 2 Thessalonians 3:3-5,13
YOUNGER KIDS: 2 Thessalonians 3:13
MEMORY VERSE: 1 Corinthians 1:18

EXPLAIN

- Paul wrote another letter to the believers in Thessalonica.
- Paul reminded them that God would guard and strengthen them.
- Paul wrote to encourage them to continue following Jesus. He also warned against not becoming tired of doing good.
- Sometimes we start something and it gets old or boring, so we start to slack off. Paul wanted to make sure that we don't do that when we follow Jesus. We should never get tired of following Jesus, and He will give us the strength we need to keep following Him.

APPLY

We should always encourage others who follow Jesus. Find the highlighted words.

A	T	E	D	J	U	O	L	D	U	Y	B	C
F	S	H	F	R	T	V	B	N	Y	J	J	K
O	O	B	E	N	C	O	U	R	A	G	E	R
L	X	Z	R	S	B	H	I	U	H	N	S	M
L	M	N	V	T	S	Y	T	R	S	D	U	B
O	B	G	T	R	M	A	B	V	C	Q	S	E
W	W	E	R	E	T	G	L	V	B	T	V	U
I	Z	S	E	N	E	R	E	O	R	T	V	H
N	T	Y	T	G	K	D	T	F	N	V	B	N
G	Q	I	W	T	R	T	T	V	U	I	J	M
C	T	V	R	H	T	Y	E	V	U	I	C	O
J	K	U	B	E	R	E	R	I	K	L	M	A
G	T	Y	U	N	D	J	G	R	E	W	H	T

RESPOND

PRAY: Jesus, please help me follow You and encourage others who follow You, too.

HIGHLIGHT

OLDER KIDS: Acts 19:1-5
YOUNGER KIDS: Acts 19:1-5
MEMORY VERSE: 1 Corinthians 1:18

EXPLAIN

- Paul traveled to a town called Ephesus.
- Paul was always talking to people about Jesus. He tried to help them understand that Jesus is the Messiah.
- Many people heard the gospel and were saved, but some people were angry with Paul. These people believed in false gods and did not want to hear the good news.
- Sometimes people will be unhappy with us for sharing the good news about Jesus. Sharing Jesus should be more important than what other people say.

APPLY

It is more important for us to please God than other people. Discuss: Is it always easy to please Jesus instead of our friends? Why or why not?

RESPOND

PRAY: Heavenly Father, please help me to follow and please You no matter what others say.

HIGHLIGHT

OLDER KIDS: 1 Corinthians 1:26-31
YOUNGER KIDS: 1 Corinthians 1:30-31
MEMORY VERSE: 1 Corinthians 1:18

EXPLAIN

- Paul wrote a letter to the believers at Corinth.
- This group of people argued between themselves, but Paul wanted them to focus on Jesus, His message, and the Holy Spirit instead.
- Paul reminded them that God's ways are higher than ours, and His wisdom is better than anything the world can offer.
- Sometimes we forget that God's ways are different than what we think. God sent the Holy Spirit to help us follow Him, so we should trust God and share about Jesus instead of arguing with other believers.

APPLY

God's ways and God's wisdom are always better than anyone else's. Write *T* next to the true statements and *F* next to the false statements:

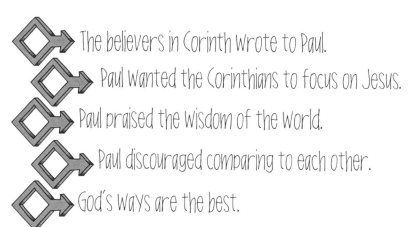

The believers in Corinth wrote to Paul.

Paul wanted the Corinthians to focus on Jesus.

Paul praised the wisdom of the world.

Paul discouraged comparing to each other.

God's ways are the best.

RESPOND

PRAY: Heavenly Father, please help me to remember that Your ways and Your wisdom are better than anyone else's.

 HIGHLIGHT

OLDER KIDS: 1 Corinthians 4:1-5
YOUNGER KIDS: 1 Corinthians 4:1-2
MEMORY VERSE: 1 Corinthians 1:18

EXPLAIN

- Paul is writing to the believers at Corinth.
- Paul says we are rulers over what God has given to us.
- Paul explains that our focus should be on making sure we are faithful to God. We should not worry about what others think of us.
- It is not our place to judge what other people are doing. That's for God to do. We are responsible to God to obey and be faithful.

APPLY

God cares about our faithfulness and our attitude. Fill in the blanks to complete 1 Corinthians 1:18.

FOR THE _____ IS

_____ , BUT

_____

_____ .

 RESPOND

PRAY: Heavenly Father, please help me to be faithful to You.

HIGHLIGHT

OLDER KIDS: 1 Corinthians 6:19-20
YOUNGER KIDS: 1 Corinthians 6:19-20
MEMORY VERSE: 1 Corinthians 13:13

EXPLAIN

- Paul's letter to the believers in Corinth continues.
- Paul wants believers to understand that we should glorify God with our body.
- We must take care of our bodies because they are a special dwelling place for the Holy Spirit.
- Our bodies are not just ours—our bodies belong to God. When we take care of the body God gave us, we glorify Him.

APPLY

We can glorify God by taking care of our bodies. List three ways you can take care of your body.

RESPOND

PRAY: Heavenly Father, please help me to take care of the body You gave me.

 **HIGHLIGHT**

OLDER KIDS: 1 Corinthians 7:23-24
YOUNGER KIDS: 1 Corinthians 7:23-24
MEMORY VERSE: 1 Corinthians 13:13

 EXPLAIN

- In his letter, Paul answered questions for the believers at Corinth.
- Paul wanted them to understand that we should serve God wherever we are.
- God wants us to serve Him anytime, anywhere. We don't have to wait until we are somewhere special to serve Him.
- Everyone has different circumstances in life, but God calls each of us to serve Him right where we are.

 APPLY

Living for God is more important than what we are going through in our lives. Start with the clock in the center and follow the directions to find each letter. Return to the clock each time. When should we start serving God?

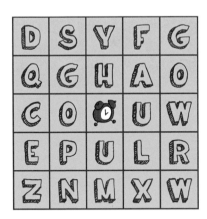

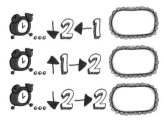

 **RESPOND**

PRAY: Heavenly Father, please help me to live for You right where I am.

HIGHLIGHT

OLDER KIDS: 1 Corinthians 9:24–27
YOUNGER KIDS: 1 Corinthians 9:24–27
MEMORY VERSE: 1 Corinthians 13:13

EXPLAIN

- Paul told the believers at Corinth that the Christian life is like a race.
- When we run a race, we run with purpose, focusing on the finish line.
- In a regular race, only one person wins the prize, but this race is for everyone who believes in Jesus. Our prize as Christians is spending forever with God.
- When Paul talks about a race, he's not talking about racing against other people. He's talking about reaching for a goal—the prize—at the end. Paul means that we should live with a purpose—following Jesus.

APPLY

Heaven is the prize for Christians who run the race. Following God should always be our purpose for running the race. Begin the maze at the shoes and work your way up to the correct answer.

RESPOND

PRAY: Heavenly Father, please help me focus on living with purpose.

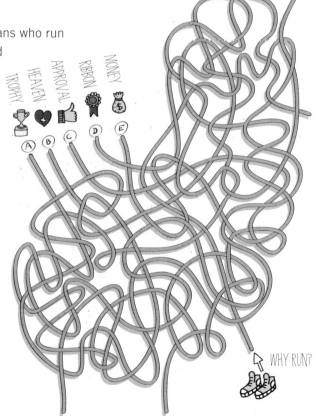

HIGHLIGHT

OLDER KIDS: 1 Corinthians 12:12-20
YOUNGER KIDS: 1 Corinthians 12:12
MEMORY VERSE: 1 Corinthians 13:13

EXPLAIN

- Paul told the believers at Corinth that we are all part of one body, or family, of Christ.
- Paul explained that as believers, we are all different with different jobs, but we are supposed to work together as a body.
- Paul says it is good that we are all different with different strengths so that we can help each other.
- Just like our feet, hands, and eyes are all different parts of our body, they all have their own special jobs. If one of them is missing or not working properly, it makes a difference to the entire body. Paul tells us that each of us is important to the body of Christ.

APPLY

God made us all different so we can be helpful in the body of Christ. Close your eyes and place your finger in this area. Then open your eyes and look at which action your finger is on. Do the action while naming some of the jobs we might have as a part of the body of Christ.

RESPOND

PRAY: Heavenly Father, thank You for making us all different. Please help me be a supportive part of Your family.

 **HIGHLIGHT**

OLDER KIDS: 1 Corinthians 13:4-7
YOUNGER KIDS: 1 Corinthians 13:4-5
MEMORY VERSE: 1 Corinthians 13:13

 EXPLAIN

- Paul wanted the believers at Corinth to understand what love means.
- Paul made it clear that if you can do lots of great things but you don't love others, those great things mean nothing. Love is the most important thing.
- All Christians and their abilities are important, but loving each other is the most important.
- Paul tells us that we can have all kinds of special talents and abilities, but if we don't know how to love, we have nothing. He also tells us what love is and how love behaves.

 APPLY

Loving others is important and helps Christians be part of the body of Christ. Create 1 Corinthians 13:13 in the boxes to the right.

 RESPOND

PRAY: Heavenly Father, thank You for loving me. Please help me to love others.

FAITH
HOPE
LOVE

LOVE

 HIGHLIGHT

OLDER KIDS: 1 Corinthians 15:58
YOUNGER KIDS: 1 Corinthians 15:58
MEMORY VERSE: Romans 1:16

 EXPLAIN

- Paul was finishing his first letter to the believers at Corinth.
- Paul's final encouragement was to remind believers to be faithful and work their hardest for God.
- Paul wanted the believers to understand that the work they do for God is important.
- Paul reminds us to be faithful in our work and strong in our faith. Everything we do for God makes a difference.

APPLY

God wants us to be faithful and always do our best. Decode: God wants me to do my _____.

THE SECOND **LETTER** IN THE ALPHABET   THE SECOND **VOWEL** IN THE ALPHABET   THE LETTER THAT FOLLOWS **R**   THE LETTER THAT FOLLOWS **S**

 **RESPOND**

PRAY: Heavenly Father, please help me be faithful and always do my best for You.

HIGHLIGHT

OLDER KIDS: 2 Corinthians 1:20-22
YOUNGER KIDS: 2 Corinthians 1:20
MEMORY VERSE: Romans 1:16

EXPLAIN

- Paul wrote another letter to the church at Corinth.
- Paul tells us that God's promises are a "yes" in Christ. We can always trust in God's promises when we trust in Jesus.
- Paul reminds us that God's promises are true, and He will always fulfill them.
- Paul wants us to see that God has kept His promises all throughout Scripture. God doesn't change—He is the same forever. We can trust that He will continue to fulfill His promises.

APPLY

God always keeps His promises, and we can trust He will fulfill them. As you color the letters, think about the promises Paul described that are a "yes" in Christ.

RESPOND

PRAY: Heavenly Father, thank You for always keeping Your promises. Help me to trust You.

HIGHLIGHT

OLDER KIDS: 2 Corinthians 4:7-10
YOUNGER KIDS: 2 Corinthians 4:7-10
MEMORY VERSE: Romans 1:16

EXPLAIN

- In this letter to the believers at Corinth, Paul wrote that Jesus shines in our hearts like a light.
- Paul says our treasure (our light) is in clay jars, and if we are broken or have hard times, Jesus' light shines through us and brings glory to God.
- Paul wants us to understand that even though we have Jesus, life will not always be easy.
- Paul used clay jars as an example because that was something everyone understood. Clay jars get broken, and whatever is inside of them shows through the cracks. Paul meant that when a person is broken, Jesus shines through their weaknesses. In that way, God gets the glory in our lives.

 APPLY

We can give glory to God and show His work in our lives even during tough times. Solve the puzzle.

 RESPOND

PRAY: Heavenly Father, help me to show Your work in my life all the time.

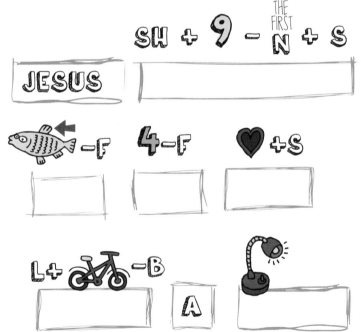

HIGHLIGHT

OLDER KIDS: 2 Corinthians 5:17-20
YOUNGER KIDS: 2 Corinthians 5:17
MEMORY VERSE: Romans 1:16

EXPLAIN

- Paul told the believers at Corinth that when Christ forgives us, He makes us new.
- Because Jesus forgave us, we should share that good news with other people.
- We are supposed to be ambassadors, or representatives, for Jesus.
- Jesus' sacrifice and forgiveness is for everyone. We should be grateful for His sacrifice for us. We should also understand that it's our job to represent Jesus and tell others about His forgiveness.

APPLY

We can show Jesus to others by the way we live. Discuss: How can you show Jesus to others around you?

RESPOND

PRAY: Heavenly Father, please help me show Jesus to others.

HIGHLIGHT

OLDER KIDS: 2 Corinthians 8:1-7
YOUNGER KIDS: 2 Corinthians 8:7
MEMORY VERSE: Romans 1:16

 EXPLAIN

- Paul shared with the believers in Corinth about the churches in Macedonia.
- Even though the churches in Macedonia were poor, they raised money for poor Christians in Jerusalem.
- Paul reminds us that Jesus taught us to give generously.
- We do not have to be rich in order to give and help others. When we are truly grateful for Jesus and His sacrifice for us, we want to be generous and help others.

 APPLY

We can be generous and give to help others. List three ways you can be generous by giving to help others.

 RESPOND

PRAY: Heavenly Father, please help me to be generous and give to help others.

HIGHLIGHT

OLDER KIDS: 2 Corinthians 9:6-8
YOUNGER KIDS: 2 Corinthians 9:7
MEMORY VERSE: Romans 5:1

EXPLAIN

- Paul challenged the believers in Corinth to give freely and cheerfully—not because someone forced them.
- God loves it when we give generously with a happy heart.
- Our cheerful giving is an example of the gospel for others to see.
- Our attitude is important when we give. When we give with a happy heart, our giving is a blessing to us and to others.

APPLY

We bring glory to God when we give with a happy heart. As you find and circle the matching pair of gifts, think about giving with a happy heart.

RESPOND

PRAY: Heavenly Father, please help me to give with a happy heart.

 **HIGHLIGHT**

OLDER KIDS: 2 Corinthians 12:9-10
YOUNGER KIDS: 2 Corinthians 12:9-10
MEMORY VERSE: Romans 5:1

 EXPLAIN

- Paul told the Corinthians about some trouble he had in his life.
- Paul asked God to take his troubles away, but instead, God gave him the grace to be able to handle the trouble.
- Paul tells us that when he has to depend on God, he's strong, because God is strong.
- God doesn't always take our troubles away. When He doesn't take them away, God will give us His grace and strength to handle the trouble.

 APPLY

God cares about our troubles. He will give us His grace and strength to be able to handle them. Follow the maze to join the beginning of each statement to its completion.

 RESPOND

PRAY: Heavenly Father, thank You for caring about me. Please give me Your grace and strength to handle any trouble.

HIGHLIGHT

OLDER KIDS: Romans 1:16-17
YOUNGER KIDS: Romans 1:16-17
MEMORY VERSE: Romans 5:1

EXPLAIN

- Paul wrote a letter to the Christians in Rome.
- Paul wanted them to understand that Jesus' salvation is for everyone, not just certain groups of people.
- Paul was not ashamed of God or His Word.
- Paul had once hated Christians, but since Jesus changed him, he told Christians that he was not ashamed of the gospel of Christ. Paul's life was changed by his faith in Jesus, and he wanted others to have the same opportunity.

APPLY

We should not be ashamed of the good news of Jesus. It's for everyone! Look at this diagram to learn how to say "Always be ready to tell what you know about Jesus" in sign language.

Always be ready to tell

What you know about Jesus.

RESPOND

PRAY: Heavenly Father, thank You that Your forgiveness is for everyone.

HIGHLIGHT

OLDER KIDS: Romans 3:21-24
YOUNGER KIDS: Romans 3:23
MEMORY VERSE: Romans 5:1

EXPLAIN

- Paul explained to Jewish people that they needed God's grace just as much as Gentiles (people who were not Jews).
- Paul told the Roman Christians that grace through faith in Jesus is the only way to salvation.
- Paul wanted to make sure they understood salvation did not come from following the Law, or the rules from the Old Testament
- Paul explained so the Jews understood that they weren't any better than the Gentiles. Everyone has sinned and needs grace and faith in Jesus to be saved.

APPLY

Who has sinned and needs faith in Jesus for salvation? Unscramble the letters to find the answer.

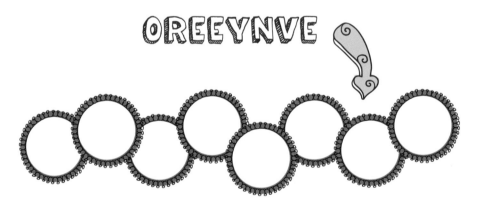

OREEYNVE

RESPOND

PRAY: Heavenly Father, thank You for offering grace and salvation for everyone through Jesus.

HIGHLIGHT

OLDER KIDS: Romans 5:6-8
YOUNGER KIDS: Romans 5:6-8
MEMORY VERSE: Romans 5:1

EXPLAIN

- Paul reminds us that Jesus died for our sin, knowing that we were sinners and couldn't save ourselves.
- God loved us so much that He sent Jesus to die for us.
- God saved us through Jesus' death and resurrection, so we can give glory to Him.
- God knew how sinful we are, but He sent Jesus to die for us anyway. God's salvation is for us. Forever.

APPLY

God gave us grace when He didn't have to, and He continues giving us grace every day. Write Romans 5:1 in the circle. Use the words around the edge of the circle to help you.

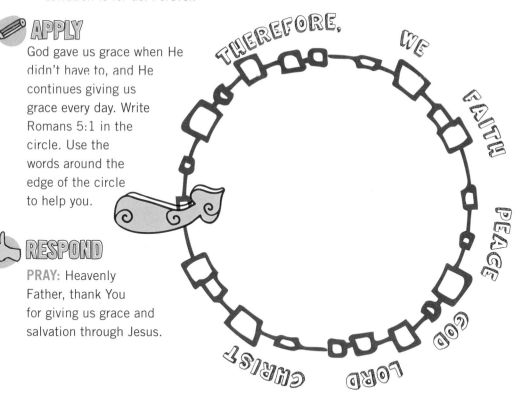

RESPOND

PRAY: Heavenly Father, thank You for giving us grace and salvation through Jesus.

 **HIGHLIGHT**
OLDER KIDS: Romans 8:28
YOUNGER KIDS: Romans 8:28
MEMORY VERSE: Romans 12:2

 EXPLAIN

- Paul continued his letter to the Romans.
- Paul tells us that through Jesus, we have the Spirit's power to help us live in a way that honors God.
- Paul shares that all things work together for the good of those who love God.
- Paul wanted Christians to understand that Jesus and the Holy Spirit give us the power to honor God with our lives. Believers are all part of God's family, and He makes all things work together for our good and His glory, even when we don't understand.

 APPLY

God works in all things for our good and His glory. Each time you see a white arrow, transfer the letter into the box below. When you see a RED arrow, switch this letter to a new letter that forms a new word. Use the pictures to give you a clue!

 RESPOND

PRAY: Heavenly Father, thank You for making all things work together for Your glory.

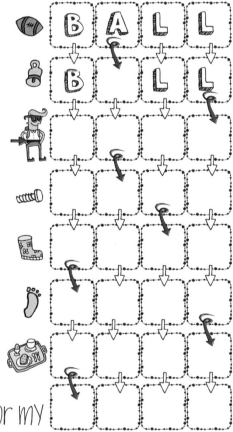

God works
in all things for my
and His glory.

HIGHLIGHT

OLDER KIDS: Romans 10:9-13
YOUNGER KIDS: Romans 10:13
MEMORY VERSE: Romans 12:2

EXPLAIN

- Paul told the Romans that we are saved by faith in Jesus alone, not by anything we do for ourselves.
- Paul explained that if we believe in Jesus with our hearts and ask Jesus to save us with our mouths, He will save us.
- God's salvation is for everyone.
- Paul wanted the Romans to understand that knowing about Jesus wasn't enough. We must truly believe in our hearts and ask Jesus to save us—and He will. Everyone who asks for salvation will receive it.

APPLY

Everyone who asks Jesus for salvation will be saved from sin. Who do you know that you could tell about Jesus' forgiveness?

RESPOND

PRAY: Heavenly Father, thank You for giving salvation to everyone who asks.

HIGHLIGHT

OLDER KIDS: Romans 12:1-2
YOUNGER KIDS: Romans 12:1-2
MEMORY VERSE: Romans 12:2

EXPLAIN

- Paul was still instructing the Romans in this letter.
- Paul tells believers that taking good care of our bodies is a way to worship God.
- Paul says believers are not supposed to be like everyone else—Christians are supposed to be different from others in the world.
- Believers are different from people who don't know Jesus because of God's love in our hearts and His Word in our minds.

APPLY

God's love will make us different from others—and that's a good thing! Write Romans 12:2 in the circle.

RESPOND

PRAY: Heavenly Father, thank You for Your love that makes me different.

HIGHLIGHT

OLDER KIDS: Romans 14:10-12
YOUNGER KIDS: Romans 14:10-12
MEMORY VERSE: Romans 12:2

EXPLAIN

- In his letter, Paul asks the Roman believers why they are being unkind to each other.
- Paul reminds them that we will all bow before God and praise Him together.
- People are accountable to God for their actions.
- Paul says we shouldn't judge each other for having different beliefs about things. We should not do anything that causes someone else to sin.

APPLY

When we love each other, we will be helpful to others. Following the path, write all the blue letters in the blue boxes, red letters in the red boxes, yellow letters in yellow boxes, and green letters in green boxes.

God wants us to be

and

We are

We shouldn't do things that encourage others to

RESPOND

PRAY: Heavenly Father, please help me to love others like You love them.

HIGHLIGHT

OLDER KIDS: Romans 15:5-6
YOUNGER KIDS: Romans 15:5-6
MEMORY VERSE: Romans 12:2

EXPLAIN

- Paul is finishing his letter to the Romans.
- Paul says that with God's power to help us, we can be kind to others.
- Paul told the Romans that when we follow God's commands and love each other, it brings glory to God.
- Paul explains that, as Christians, we are to love each other because Jesus loves us. When we love each other, we can focus our attention to bringing glory to God together.

APPLY

Unscramble the words below to find out what happens when we love others.

OVLE   GSRIBN   YRGOL

When we ( ) each other, it ( ) ( ) to God.

RESPOND

PRAY: Heavenly Father, please help me to love others and bring glory to You.

WEEK 46

DAY 1

HIGHLIGHT

OLDER KIDS: Acts 20:7-12
YOUNGER KIDS: Acts 20:9-10,12
MEMORY VERSE: 2 Corinthians 4:7

EXPLAIN

- Paul was in Troas preparing to leave, so he wanted to preach to the people one more time.
- While Paul was preaching, a young man was sitting in the window and fell asleep. The young man fell out of the window and died.
- Paul went down to the boy and wrapped his arms around him. God had brought the boy back to life!
- Paul didn't just preach—he helped people, too. God allowed Paul to do miracles in order to bring glory to Himself.

APPLY

God helps people through miracles. Follow the paths to find out what God has.

GOD HAS

RESPOND

PRAY: Heavenly Father, thank You for having power over death.

HIGHLIGHT · EXPLAIN · APPLY · RESPOND   READING #226   231

 HIGHLIGHT

OLDER KIDS: Acts 23:11
YOUNGER KIDS: Acts 23:11
MEMORY VERSE: 2 Corinthians 4:7

EXPLAIN

- In Rome, some people wanted to hurt Paul because he was preaching about Jesus.
- Paul was a Roman citizen, which meant the Roman soldiers gave him special treatment.
- God told Paul to be courageous because he would tell people the good news in Rome.
- The Roman soldiers took special care of Paul since he was born in Rome. God told Paul he would preach in Rome, even when people wanted to kill him there.

 APPLY

God is always at work and will give us the strength we need to live for Him. As you figure out where each puzzle piece fits, write the text in the space.

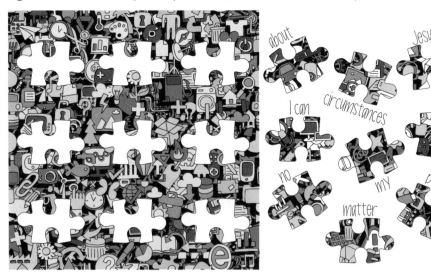

 **RESPOND**

PRAY: Heavenly Father, thank You for giving me the strength to live for You.

HIGHLIGHT

OLDER KIDS: Acts 24:14-16
YOUNGER KIDS: Acts 24:14-16
MEMORY VERSE: 2 Corinthians 4:7

EXPLAIN

- Paul was arrested and put in prison once again.
- The Roman governors didn't know what to do with Paul. They didn't think he had done anything wrong.
- Paul told people about Jesus no matter where he was—even in prison.
- Paul took every chance he had to share the good news about Jesus with other people. God allowed Paul to experience many different places and situations so people could hear about Jesus.

APPLY

We can tell people about Jesus no matter what circumstances we are in. Begin in the center, following the directions to discover the answer to this question: When can I tell others about Jesus?

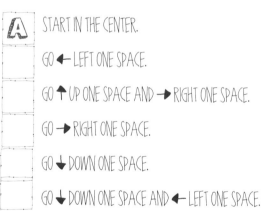

A | START IN THE CENTER.

GO ← LEFT ONE SPACE.

GO ↑ UP ONE SPACE AND → RIGHT ONE SPACE.

GO → RIGHT ONE SPACE.

GO ↓ DOWN ONE SPACE.

GO ↓ DOWN ONE SPACE AND ← LEFT ONE SPACE.

RESPOND

PRAY: Heavenly Father, please help me to tell others about You.

HIGHLIGHT

OLDER KIDS: Acts 27:20-26
YOUNGER KIDS: Acts 27:23-24
MEMORY VERSE: 2 Corinthians 4:7

EXPLAIN

- Paul was sailing on a ship as a prisoner headed to Rome to go before Caesar, the ruler of Rome.
- The ship was caught in a terrible storm, and everyone was afraid they would die.
- God sent an angel to tell Paul that he and everyone on the ship would be safe.
- Paul was faithful to follow God. God never left Paul. We can see that God stays faithful all the time.

APPLY

God never leaves us. He is always faithful to us. Use the flag code below to decode this message.

RESPOND

PRAY: Heavenly Father, thank You for never leaving me.

 **HIGHLIGHT**

OLDER KIDS: Acts 28:23-24
YOUNGER KIDS: Acts 28:23-24
MEMORY VERSE: 2 Corinthians 4:7

 EXPLAIN

- Paul's ship had finally arrived in Rome.
- Paul was allowed to live in a house as a prisoner, and people could come visit him.
- Even though he was a prisoner, Paul still told people the good news about Jesus.
- Paul had endured some really tough times, and he spent a lot of time as a prisoner. He didn't feel sorry for himself or have a bad attitude, though. He kept telling people about God's love every chance he got.

 APPLY

We should tell people about Jesus every chance we get. Fill in the blanks to complete 2 Corinthians 4:7.

_____ THIS TREASURE

IN_____ ,

_____ POWER

_____ GOD

_____ US.

 **RESPOND**

PRAY: Heavenly Father, please help me tell people about Jesus.

HIGHLIGHT

OLDER KIDS: Colossians 2:6-7
YOUNGER KIDS: Colossians 2:6-7
MEMORY VERSES: Ephesians 2:8-9

EXPLAIN

- Paul wrote a letter to the church at Colossae while he was in prison in Rome.
- Some people were teaching wrong things about God, and Paul wanted the church at Colossae to know the truth.
- Paul wanted them to understand that faith in Jesus is the only way to salvation.
- Some teachers were teaching false things about worshiping God. Our faith is in Jesus, and we should always follow Him. We should focus on what Jesus wants and not what we want.

APPLY

Jesus is the source of our salvation, not other people or our actions. Find the way to salvation through this maze.

SALVATION

RESPOND

PRAY: Jesus, thank You for being the source of my salvation!

HIGHLIGHT

OLDER KIDS: Colossians 3:12-17
YOUNGER KIDS: Colossians 3:12-13
MEMORY VERSES: Ephesians 2:8-9

EXPLAIN

- Paul wanted to help believers know how they should act.
- Paul told believers that as followers of Christ, our behavior will show we believe. We should have godly characteristics that set us apart from others.
- Paul said that everything we do should be for God's glory.
- He explained that our salvation does not depend on our actions, but if we are true followers of Christ, our actions will show it. We will show the same kind of love Jesus did.

APPLY

If we love Jesus and follow Him, our actions will show it. Find words in the puzzle that show we are followers of Christ. Use Colossians 3:12 for some hints!

RESPOND

PRAY: Heavenly Father, please help me to show love like Jesus did.

NEED HELP? compassion, forgiveness, patience, peace, thankfulness, honesty, humility, love, gentleness

HIGHLIGHT

OLDER KIDS: Ephesians 2:8-10
YOUNGER KIDS: Ephesians 2:8-10
MEMORY VERSES: Ephesians 2:8-9

EXPLAIN

- Paul wrote a letter to the church at Ephesus.
- Paul reminds believers that we are saved because of God's grace. Salvation is His gift to us.
- Paul told the Ephesians that we are God's creation, and He created us for a good purpose.
- Paul reminds us salvation is a gift from God. There is nothing for us to be proud of—God deserves all the glory. He created us and has a good purpose for us.

APPLY

God has a good purpose for each of us. Using the words as clues, write Ephesians 2:8-9 in the box.

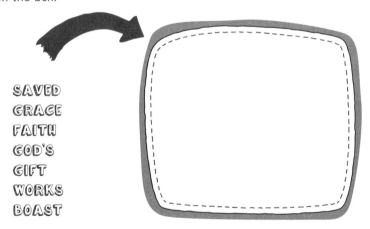

SAVED
GRACE
FAITH
GOD'S
GIFT
WORKS
BOAST

RESPOND

PRAY: Heavenly Father, thank You for creating me for a good purpose.

HIGHLIGHT

OLDER KIDS: Ephesians 4:25-32
YOUNGER KIDS: Ephesians 4:25-26
MEMORY VERSES: Ephesians 2:8-9

EXPLAIN

- Paul wanted the church at Ephesus to know how they should act as followers of Jesus.
- Paul reminded believers that before they knew Jesus, they acted one way. Now that Jesus had changed them, they should act differently.
- We should think about the way Jesus loves and forgives others so we can do the same.
- When we didn't understand Jesus' love, we sinned. After we come to know Jesus, we should act out of His love. We will act differently because of our love for Jesus.

APPLY

Our actions should be different because of Jesus' love. Discuss: How do you think sin makes us act? How do we act when we act out of Jesus' love?

RESPOND

PRAY: Heavenly Father, please help me to love like Jesus loves.

HIGHLIGHT

OLDER KIDS: Ephesians 6:1-4
YOUNGER KIDS: Ephesians 6:1-4
MEMORY VERSES: Ephesians 2:8-9

EXPLAIN

- Paul continued talking to the church at Ephesus about how they should treat others.
- Paul gave families instructions about how to treat one another.
- Paul said that children should obey their parents just as they would obey God, and they will be blessed if they do.
- Paul took time to talk about how we should treat each other, but he talked about families because families are so important. Husbands and wives, children and parents—everyone is supposed to love and respect one another.

 APPLY

We will be blessed when we honor our parents. List three ways you can honor your parents.

RESPOND

PRAY: Heavenly Father, please help me to love and respect others.

HIGHLIGHT

OLDER KIDS: Philippians 1:20
YOUNGER KIDS: Philippians 1:20
MEMORY VERSE: Philippians 3:7

EXPLAIN

- Paul wrote to the church at Philippi from a Roman prison.
- Paul told them that he was certain that being in prison had given more people the chance to hear about Jesus.
- Paul's hope was that he would not be ashamed of the gospel and Christ would be honored because of him.
- Paul's life was not easy, but he knew that many people heard the good news because of him. His life goal was to honor God, not have an easy life.

APPLY

We can glorify God with our lives no matter where we are. Beginning at the bottom, find your way through each level of the maze using ladders and stairs. As you go, collect the words you find.

RESPOND

PRAY: Heavenly Father, please help me to glorify You no matter where I am.

HIGHLIGHT

OLDER KIDS: Philippians 4:11-13
YOUNGER KIDS: Philippians 4:13
MEMORY VERSE: Philippians 3:7

EXPLAIN

- Paul was finishing his letter to the Philippians.
- Paul told them he has learned to be satisfied with whatever he has in every circumstance.
- Paul said the secret to being content is knowing Christ will give you the strength to do what God wants you to do.
- Paul had a lot of things at one time, and there were times he had very few things. He did not need material things to be happy because he knew God would provide him with the strength to do His will.

APPLY

God will give us the strength to follow Him and do His will. God will give me _____ to follow Him. Find the missing word by drawing a line between each matching pair of pictures. Each line will pass through a letter. Write the letter in the box to solve.

 RESPOND

PRAY: Heavenly Father, thank You for giving me the strength to follow You and do Your will.

HIGHLIGHT
OLDER KIDS: Hebrews 2:18
YOUNGER KIDS: Hebrews 2:18
MEMORY VERSE: Philippians 3:7

EXPLAIN

- The writer of Hebrews wanted to encourage Christians to keep following Jesus.
- The writer wanted believers to understand why Jesus became a man and died for us.
- Jesus became a man and died so that we can be saved from our sin and be with God.
- God used to speak through prophets, but then He sent Jesus and spoke through Him. Jesus knows what it's like to be a man on earth—He came to earth to pay the price for our sin.

APPLY

Jesus came to save us from our sin. Complete each word by filling the missing letters in the red boxes. When you are finished, read the message in the red boxes.

RESPOND

PRAY: Jesus, thank You for coming to pay the price for my sin.

OLDER KIDS: Hebrews 4:12-13
YOUNGER KIDS: Hebrews 4:12-13
MEMORY VERSE: Philippians 3:7

 EXPLAIN

- The writer of Hebrews reminds us that God's Word is powerful.
- Hebrews says that God's Word is true and speaks to our hearts and every part of our lives.
- God's Word reminds us that we can't hide anything from God, and He knows the truth about us.
- The writer says that we have to answer to God for our actions. God knows everything about us, and He loves us anyway. To be forgiven from our sin, we just have to ask Him. He will forgive anyone who asks.

 APPLY

God's Word and its truth are for everyone. Fill in the blanks to complete Philippians 3:7.

BUT _____ .

I _____

_____ LOSS

_____ OF CHRIST.

 RESPOND

PRAY: Heavenly Father, thank You for Your Word and its truth.

HIGHLIGHT

OLDER KIDS: Hebrews 6:10-12
YOUNGER KIDS: Hebrews 6:10-12
MEMORY VERSE: Philippians 3:7

EXPLAIN

- The writer of Hebrews encouraged believers to keep growing in their faith.
- Hebrews tells us that we can't just hope we grow in our faith in God—we have to work at it on purpose.
- The writer suggests that we can look to people who are good examples of strong Christians and learn from them.
- It is important to continue following Jesus and growing in our faith. If we don't purposely try to grow, we will stay like spiritual babies instead of growing up in our faith.

APPLY

Growing in our faith is important. Discuss: What does it mean to be an example? Who is a good example for you?

RESPOND

PRAY: Heavenly Father, please help me to grow in my faith.

HIGHLIGHT

OLDER KIDS: Hebrews 7:24-25
YOUNGER KIDS: Hebrews 7:24-25
MEMORY VERSE: 2 Corinthians 5:17

EXPLAIN

- The writer of Hebrews compared the high priest from the tribe of Levi to Jesus, our High Priest.
- Jesus is the Son of God, and His work as High Priest is forever, not like the priests of the Old Testament.
- The sacrifice Jesus made when He died for our salvation lasts forever.
- The sacrifices the Old Testament high priests made for people's sin didn't last. They were offering sacrifices as people who were sinners. Because Jesus never sinned and He is the Son of God, His sacrifice lasts forever.

APPLY

The salvation Jesus gives us never fades or goes away. Connect the beginning of each sentence to its completion.

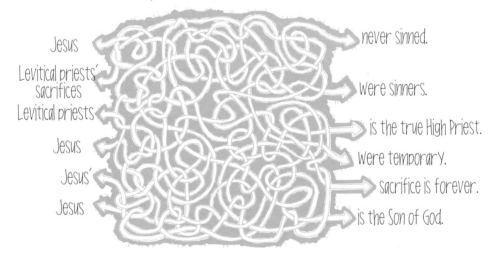

Jesus
Levitical priests' sacrifices
Levitical priests
Jesus
Jesus'
Jesus

never sinned.
were sinners.
is the true High Priest.
were temporary.
sacrifice is forever.
is the Son of God.

RESPOND

PRAY: Jesus, thank You for salvation that lasts forever.

OLDER KIDS: Hebrews 9:11-12
YOUNGER KIDS: Hebrews 9:11-12
MEMORY VERSE: 2 Corinthians 5:17

 EXPLAIN

- The writer of Hebrews compares God's Old Testament Law and the tabernacle during Moses' time.
- The priests would sprinkle blood from the animal sacrifices, following God's instructions for the sacrifices.
- The priests had to make sacrifices over and over, but Jesus' sacrifice lasts forever.
- We can see the difference between the sacrifice of animals and the sacrifice Jesus gave—Himself. The animal sacrifices didn't last, but Jesus' sacrifice of His own innocent blood lasts forever. We can trust that when Jesus forgives us, our sins are forgiven forever.

 APPLY

Because He is holy, Jesus' sacrifice lasts forever. Fill in the blanks to complete 2 Corinthians 5:17.

THEREFORE, IF_____ IN CHRIST,

_____ NEW _____;

_____

_____ .

 **RESPOND**

PRAY: Jesus, thank You for Your sacrifice for me.

HIGHLIGHT

OLDER KIDS: Hebrews 10:23-25
YOUNGER KIDS: Hebrews 10:23-25
MEMORY VERSE: 2 Corinthians 5:17

EXPLAIN

- Hebrews tells us that, because Jesus is our High Priest, we can be sure that He will forgive our sin.
- We can trust in God's promises so that we can focus on loving others and doing good things.
- We should encourage each other and spend time together in fellowship on a regular basis.
- We can depend on our salvation and God's promises. That gives us the opportunity to meet together and love and encourage each other.

APPLY

We can be sure of God's promises and Jesus' salvation. Use the clues to complete the puzzle.

RESPOND

PRAY: Jesus, thank You for Your sacrifice for me.

People in the Bible who lived by faith can be an _____ to us.

We may not see all of these happen

It takes faith to do this

We can do this even though we don't see

We must have this to please God

This is what we know God's promises are

The name of the book today's reading came from

It takes faith to do this

HIGHLIGHT

OLDER KIDS: Hebrews 11:1-3
YOUNGER KIDS: Hebrews 11:1-3
MEMORY VERSE: 2 Corinthians 5:17

EXPLAIN

- Hebrews teaches us that having faith means we may not get to see all of God's promises happen, but we still know they are true.
- God wants us to have faith in Him and His promises.
- The writer of Hebrews gives many examples of people in the Bible who lived by faith.
- Real faith is when we obey God and trust Him with our lives. It takes faith to obey God and follow Him.

APPLY

We can believe God, even when we don't see all His promises happen. That's faith. Name three things that you believe even though you do not see them. Here are a couple ideas to get you started: time, sound waves, emotions. Ask a parent if you get stuck.

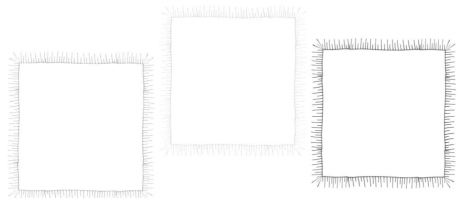

RESPOND

PRAY: Heavenly Father, please help me have faith in You.

HIGHLIGHT

OLDER KIDS: Hebrews 12:1-2
YOUNGER KIDS: Hebrews 12:1-2
MEMORY VERSE: 2 Corinthians 5:17

EXPLAIN

- The writer of Hebrews tells us life is like a race—a long race.
- Running a long race takes endurance (strength for a long time), and we have to keep our eyes on Jesus.
- Jesus suffered while focusing on what was coming—heaven.
- To run with endurance means we should keep going and depend on God for our strength. Jesus is the source of our salvation, so we should keep our eyes on Him and focus on what's coming—heaven.

APPLY

We should keep our eyes on Jesus through our whole lives. Divide the grid into four sections, each section containing four squares. Each section must contain each word in the definition of *endurance*: STRENGTH | FOR A | LONG | TIME

RESPOND

PRAY: Heavenly Father, please help me keep my eyes on You all the time.

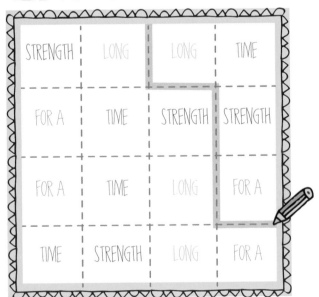

WEEK 50
DAY 1

HIGHLIGHT

OLDER KIDS: 1 Timothy 3:1-4
YOUNGER KIDS: 1 Timothy 3:1-4
MEMORY VERSE: 2 Timothy 2:15

EXPLAIN

- Paul wrote a letter to his friend Timothy.
- Paul gave Timothy instructions for being a good leader.
- Paul stated that a good leader should be kind, fair, honest, and faithful.
- Timothy was leading a church, and Paul wanted to help him be a good leader. The qualities Paul says a good leader should have are meant for everyone.

APPLY

The Bible tells us how to be a good leader. Write a check mark next to the ways this Bible passage describes a good leader.

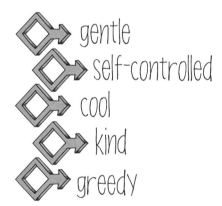

popular
fair
faithful
smart
generous

gentle
self-controlled
cool
kind
greedy

 RESPOND

PRAY: Heavenly Father, thank You for giving me instructions in Your Word on how I can be a good leader.

HIGHLIGHT · EXPLAIN · APPLY · RESPOND   READING #246   251

HIGHLIGHT

OLDER KIDS: 1 Timothy 4:11-12
YOUNGER KIDS: 1 Timothy 4:12
MEMORY VERSE: 2 Timothy 2:15

EXPLAIN

- Paul continued giving Timothy instructions for leading well.
- Paul wanted Timothy to know that even if he was young, he could make a difference for Jesus.
- We can be a good example to others by the way we speak and act.
- Paul wanted Timothy to be a good leader in his church. He gave Timothy instructions for leading and teaching others to be good leaders, too. Paul wanted to make sure Timothy understood how to act and treat others so he would be a good teacher for his church.

APPLY

We don't have to wait until we grow up to be a good example to others. Decode the message below by replacing each letter with the letter that comes before it in the alphabet.

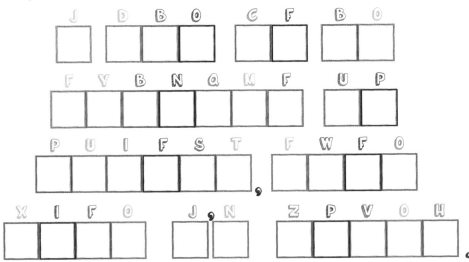

RESPOND

PRAY: Heavenly Father, please help me to be a good example to others.

HIGHLIGHT

OLDER KIDS: 2 Timothy 2:15
YOUNGER KIDS: 2 Timothy 2:15
MEMORY VERSE: 2 Timothy 2:15

EXPLAIN

- Paul wrote another letter to Timothy.
- Paul reminded Timothy to keep growing in his faith and following God.
- Paul didn't want Timothy to get discouraged but to keep on teaching others.
- Paul was in prison in Rome and thought this might be his last chance to send a message to Timothy. The things he wanted to say were not sad. He encouraged Timothy to be strong in his faith in God and always to teach others about Jesus.

APPLY

We should always live in a way that makes God happy. List three things that make God happy.

RESPOND

PRAY: Heavenly Father, thank You for people who encourage me to follow You.

HIGHLIGHT

OLDER KIDS: 2 Timothy 3:13-17
YOUNGER KIDS: 2 Timothy 3:16-17
MEMORY VERSE: 2 Timothy 2:15

EXPLAIN

- Paul told Timothy he would meet lots of people who are evil.
- Paul wanted Timothy to remember what he had been taught since he was a child—the Word of God.
- Paul reminded Timothy that Scripture is the Word of God. We need it to help us be more holy and like Jesus.
- Paul warned Timothy to be careful of evil people. Paul warned Timothy not to participate in bad behavior but to remember the things he had been taught since he was young. God's Word is the best thing to help us learn how to grow in our faith and become more holy.

APPLY

God's Word helps us grow in our faith. Use the letters around the edge of the circle to help you write 2 Timothy 2:15 inside it.

RESPOND

PRAY: Heavenly Father, thank You for giving me Your Word to help me grow in my faith and be more like You.

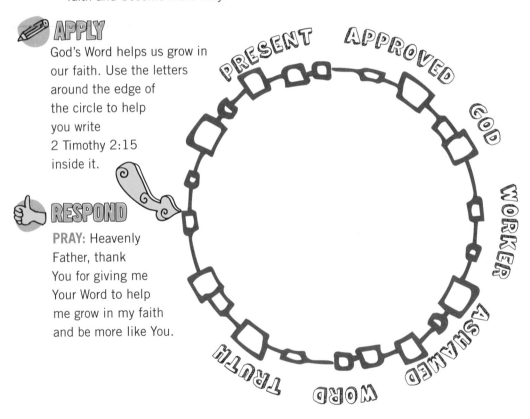

PRESENT APPROVED GOD WORKER ASHAMED WORD TRUTH

HIGHLIGHT

OLDER KIDS: 1 Peter 1:13-16
YOUNGER KIDS: 1 Peter 1:13-16
MEMORY VERSE: 2 Timothy 2:15

EXPLAIN

- Peter wrote a letter to Christians who were being persecuted (being treated badly) for their belief in Jesus.
- Peter reminded them that their hope is in Christ, not their circumstances.
- Peter told them that believers are called by God to be holy.
- Christians were being persecuted all over Rome. Peter wrote to encourage them to be faithful even during persecution. He wanted them to understand a believer's true home is heaven.

APPLY

We should follow God even in tough times.
Discuss: What does it mean to be persecuted for your faith in God?

RESPOND

PRAY: Heavenly Father, please help me always to follow You, even in tough times.

DAY 1

HIGHLIGHT

OLDER KIDS: 1 Peter 4:8-11
YOUNGER KIDS: 1 Peter 4:8-11
MEMORY VERSE: 1 John 4:11

EXPLAIN

- Peter continued his letter by telling Christians how to treat others.
- Peter said believers should love and care for each other without complaining.
- God provides the strength and ability for us to care for others, and it glorifies Him when we take care of each other.
- Peter wrote to Christians who were being persecuted for their faith. Instead of telling them to hide, Peter told them to keep following Jesus. He also wanted them to keep loving and caring for others so they could glorify God.

APPLY

We can give glory to God by loving and caring for others. Discuss: How can you care for others without complaining?

RESPOND

PRAY: Heavenly Father, please help me to glorify You by loving and caring for other people.

256   READING #251   HIGHLIGHT · EXPLAIN · APPLY · RESPOND

HIGHLIGHT

OLDER KIDS: 1 Peter 5:5-7
YOUNGER KIDS: 1 Peter 5:5-7
MEMORY VERSE: 1 John 4:11

EXPLAIN

- Peter finished this letter by telling believers to be humble.
- He said that being humble means not thinking about yourself and putting the needs of others before your own.
- Peter wrote that humility (being humble) helps us depend on God and thank Him for how He provides for us.
- Peter really wanted believers to be humble. He knew that as Christians were being persecuted, humility would be an important part of helping them depend on God.

APPLY

Putting others' needs before our own, with a happy heart, brings glory to God. List three ways you can put someone else's needs before your own.

RESPOND

PRAY: Heavenly Father, please help me to be humble and depend on You.

HIGHLIGHT

OLDER KIDS: 2 Peter 3:17-18
YOUNGER KIDS: 2 Peter 3:17-18
MEMORY VERSE: 1 John 4:11

EXPLAIN

- Peter wrote another letter to believers.
- Peter warned them about people who would try to teach wrong things about Jesus.
- Peter wanted everyone to grow in their faith and be ready for Jesus when He returns.
- Peter encouraged believers to grow in their relationship with God. He alerted them to watch out for people who would try to trick them into believing wrong things. We know Jesus will return, but we aren't sure when, so we must be ready for Him every day.

APPLY

 Jesus will come back one day, and we want to be ready when He returns. Watch out for people who try to teach wrong things about Jesus. Complete the maze without getting caught by any tricks!

RESPOND

PRAY: Heavenly Father, please help me to grow in my faith and be ready for Jesus to return.

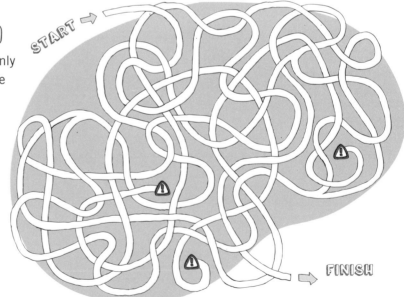

 **HIGHLIGHT**

OLDER KIDS: 1 John 1:5-9
YOUNGER KIDS: 1 John 1:9
MEMORY VERSE: 1 John 4:11

 EXPLAIN

- John wrote this letter to help believers understand Jesus really is the Son of God.
- John used light and dark to help believers understand what having a relationship with Jesus is like versus living in sin.
- John reminds Christians that if we confess our sin to God, He will forgive us.
- John was an apostle of Jesus and wrote to help believers understand who Jesus is. We show we know Jesus by obeying Him and loving others like He did.

 APPLY

God is faithful to forgive our sin when we ask. Connect the dots to remind you that God is light.

 RESPOND

PRAY: Heavenly Father, thank You for forgiving me when I ask.

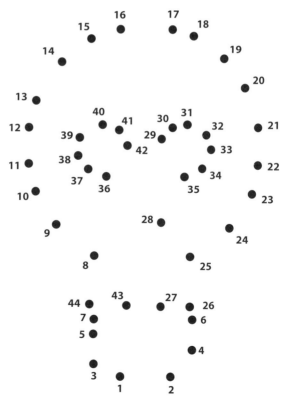

HIGHLIGHT

OLDER KIDS: 1 John 4:7-12
YOUNGER KIDS: 1 John 4:11
MEMORY VERSE: 1 John 4:11

EXPLAIN

- John talked about God's love for us. He told the early Christians that they should love each other because God loves them.
- John said that love is from God.
- God loved us first, and He sent Jesus to die for us.
- These verses remind us that before we loved God, He loved us. He even sent His own Son to be the sacrifice for our sin. We should be obedient to God, love God, and love others.

APPLY

Because God loves us, we should love others. Write 1 John 4:11 in the circle.

RESPOND

PRAY: Heavenly Father, thank You for loving me. Please help me to love others.

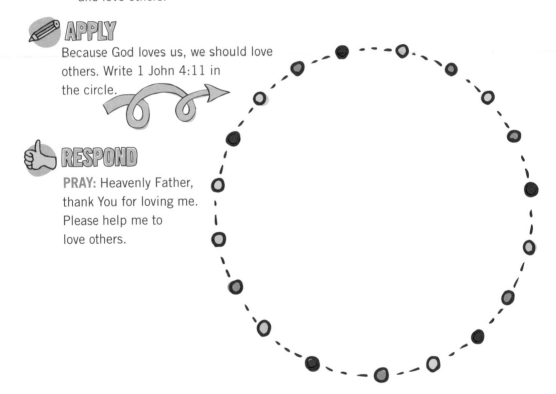

HIGHLIGHT

OLDER KIDS: Revelation 1:17-19
YOUNGER KIDS: Revelation 1:17-19
MEMORY VERSE: Revelation 3:19

EXPLAIN

- The apostle John wrote Revelation to tell believers about the vision he had from God.
- Jesus is alive today, and He has conquered death.
- God sent a special message through John about what will happen when Jesus returns.
- John was living on the island of Patmos in exile (he was forced to leave his home). Through a vision, God gave John a message for the seven churches and showed John what would happen when Jesus comes back to earth.

APPLY

Jesus is alive and will return one day and make all things new. Color the words to help you remember this truth today.

RESPOND

PRAY: Jesus, thank You for defeating death.

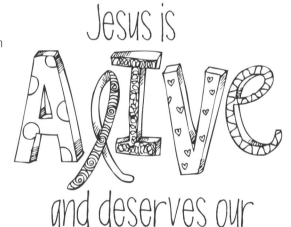

HIGHLIGHT

OLDER KIDS: Revelation 2:7
YOUNGER KIDS: Revelation 2:7
MEMORY VERSE: Revelation 3:19

EXPLAIN

- Jesus gave John messages to seven different churches.
- The messages Jesus gave for the seven churches are for all of us, too.
- The message for each church was different, but Jesus called them all to be strong in their faith.
- Jesus wants us to pay attention to the messages He gave to the seven churches. Jesus wants us to stay faithful in following Him no matter how we feel or how hard or easy our lives are.

 APPLY

Decode the message by placing the first letter of each picture in the box above it.

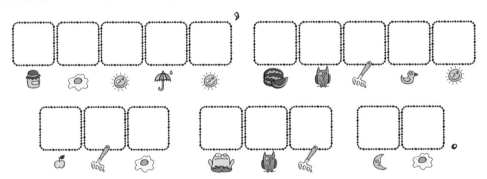

 RESPOND

PRAY: Jesus, please help me to hear Your message and be faithful to You.

 **HIGHLIGHT**

OLDER KIDS: Revelation 4:11
YOUNGER KIDS: Revelation 4:11
MEMORY VERSE: Revelation 3:19

 **EXPLAIN**

- John described what he saw in God's throne room.
- John saw many people and creatures worshiping God.
- God created all things, and He is worthy of our praise.
- John saw many things in his vision, but one was the throne of God with continuous worship of God. John may not have understood everything he saw, but he did understand that God is worthy of praise, glory, and honor.

 APPLY

God is worthy of praise, glory, and honor. Discuss: What does it mean to give God praise, glory, and honor?

 RESPOND

PRAY: Heavenly Father, thank You for being worthy of praise, glory, and honor. Please help me to worship You.

HIGHLIGHT
OLDER KIDS: Revelation 19:11-13
YOUNGER KIDS: Revelation 19:11-13
MEMORY VERSE: Revelation 3:19

EXPLAIN
- John described Jesus returning as a mighty King who will defeat evil.
- John described Jesus as riding a white horse and gives descriptions of His power and character.
- Jesus is faithful, true, and righteous.
- Jesus came the first time as a baby. When He returns, He will come as a mighty King, ready to battle against Satan and his army. We know that Jesus will defeat Satan and the forces of evil.

APPLY
Because we know Jesus will win over evil, we should share His good news with everyone. Complete Revelation 3:19 by filling in the missing words and phrases.

RESPOND
PRAY: Jesus, thank You for defeating evil. Help me share Your good news with everyone.

_____ I LOVE

I _____ AND

_____

_____ AND

REPENT.

HIGHLIGHT

OLDER KIDS: Revelation 21:5-7
YOUNGER KIDS: Revelation 21:5-7
MEMORY VERSE: Revelation 3:19

EXPLAIN

- John saw a vision of a new heaven and a new earth.
- In John's vision, Satan, death, and evil have all been judged and sent away. People who chose not to believe in Jesus have been sent to their eternal punishment.
- God is the Alpha and Omega—beginning and end. God was at the beginning, and He will be here forever. He wants everyone to know about Him, so He wants us to tell people about Him.
- When Jesus returns and defeats all evil, there will be a new heaven and a new earth. Jesus will make things new and holy once and for all.

APPLY

God is the Alpha and Omega—beginning and end. He has defeated evil and will reign forever. The Greek alphabet is different than our English alphabet. Check out the Greek alphabet below. Circle the letters ALPHA and OMEGA. Do you see why God is called the Alpha and Omega—beginning and end? What do you think that means?

RESPOND

PRAY: Heavenly Father, thank You for being the Alpha and Omega.

CHURCH TEACHING PLAN

Use this teaching plan if your church wants a weekly kids' small group focused on *Foundations for Kids*. You can group all of your kids together or divide into Younger Kids and Older Kids. *Foundations for Kids* is written for 52 weeks of Bible study, 5 days per week. Your meeting could be set up to review what kids have read the week before or to preview what they will read on their own in the week ahead.

Remember that the focus of the Foundations curriculum goes through the H.E.A.R. model. The acronym H.E.A.R. stands for Highlight, Explain, Apply, and Respond. Each of these four steps contributes to creating an atmosphere to hear God speak. Notice that all of the words in the H.E.A.R. formula are action words: Highlight, Explain, Apply, and Respond. Structure each meeting to go through the H.E.A.R. formula.

 **HIGHLIGHT**

Each week, there will be 5 passages for Younger Kids to read and 5 passages for Older Kids to read, plus a memory verse for the week. The passages always overlap and are written to the same Bible truth. Each week your meeting should ...

- **READ THE BIBLE PASSAGES.** God speaks through the Bible, when you pray, and through fellowship with others — all ways your child can hear God speak as you go through *Foundations for Kids*.
- **MEMORIZE THE WEEKLY VERSE.** Play a variety of Bible memory games where you write each word of the verse on a card, and the kids put the verse in order. You can hide cards throughout the room, run a relay race to put the cards together, make them into a puzzle, or turn over a card each time the kids say the verse.

 EXPLAIN

Each day, Explain will have 4 bullets summarizing what happened in the verse and what the verse means. Explain each passage as you read it so kids can review what happened and make connections to their experience. Always make time for kids to ask questions.

 APPLY

Every day, kids will have a learning activity to help them apply the Bible truth. This will make learning active and fun to complete these together as a group.

 **RESPOND**

Give kids a few moments to respond in personal prayer, journal, or pray together as a group. Encourage kids to remember that prayer is part of a conversation with God.

GENERAL TIPS

1. Open every session by modeling how kids can pray before they have a quiet time with God. Pray and ask God to be with your time together and to speak to you.
2. Treat the Bible with respect and affirm its trustworthiness, authority, and reliability.
3. Ask kids what they think the passage means. Read together through Explain but be open to what each child is learning and how God speaks to the kids in your group.
4. Affirm that God loves and wants to have a relationship with each child.
5. Encourage kids any time they are able to complete their reading assignments outside of your time together.

WEEK 1	WEEK 3	WEEK 5	WEEK 7	WEEK 9
OLDER SCRIPTURE	OLDER SCRIPTURE	OLDER SCRIPTURE	OLDER SCRIPTURE	OLDER SCRIPTURE
Genesis 1:27-2:2	Genesis 18:9-15	Genesis 39:21-23	Exodus 9:1-7	Exodus 32:1, 7-8
Genesis 3:8-13	Genesis 21:1-5	Genesis 41:38-42	Exodus 11:1, 4-8	Exodus 34:1-4
Genesis 7:1-6	Gen. 22:1-2, 9-12	Genesis 42:5-8	Exodus 12:12-14	Exodus 40:34-38
Genesis 9:12-17	Genesis 24:12-15	Genesis 45:3-8	Exodus 14:21-28	Leviticus 9:22-24
Job 1:6-12, 22	Genesis 25:27-34	Genesis 46:1-6	Exodus 16:11-15	Leviticus 16:15-16
YOUNGER SCRIPTURE	YOUNGER SCRIPTURE	YOUNGER SCRIPTURE	YOUNGER SCRIPTURE	YOUNGER SCRIPTURE
Genesis 1:31-2:2	Genesis 18:13-14	Genesis 39:22	Exodus 9:1-3	Exodus 32:1, 7-8
Genesis 3:8-10	Genesis 21:1-3	Genesis 41:39-41	Exodus 11:1, 4-5	Exodus 34:1-2
Genesis 7:1-5	Genesis 22:9-12	Genesis 42:5-6	Exodus 12:12-13	Exodus 40:34-35
Genesis 9:13-15	Genesis 24:14-15	Genesis 45:3-5	Exodus 14:21-22	Leviticus 9:22-23
Job 1:8-12, 22	Genesis 25:29-34	Genesis 46:5-6	Exodus 16:11-12	Leviticus 16:16
MEMORY VERSE:	MEMORY VERSE:	MEMORY VERSE:	MEMORY VERSE:	MEMORY VERSE:
Genesis 1:27	Romans 4:20	Romans 8:28	John 1:29	Matthew 22:37-38

WEEK 2	WEEK 4	WEEK 6	WEEK 8	WEEK 10
OLDER SCRIPTURE	OLDER SCRIPTURE	OLDER SCRIPTURE	OLDER SCRIPTURE	OLDER SCRIPTURE
Job 38:1-7	Genesis 28:10-15	Genesis 48:8-12	Exodus 20:1-17	Leviticus 23:1-3
Job 42:1-6, 10	Genesis 29:21-28	Exodus 50:15-21	Exodus 25:1-9	Leviticus 26:3-8
Genesis 12:1-5a	Genesis 32:24-30	Ex. 1:8-10, 2:5-10	Exodus 26:31-35	Numbers 11:1-3
Genesis 15:2-6	Genesis 33:4-9	Exodus 4:10-15	Exodus 29:38-42	Numbers 13:26-29
Genesis 17:1-8	Genesis 37:23-28	Exodus 6:6-9	Ex. 31:12-13, 16-17	Numbers 16:46-50
YOUNGER SCRIPTURE	YOUNGER SCRIPTURE	YOUNGER SCRIPTURE	YOUNGER SCRIPTURE	YOUNGER SCRIPTURE
Job 38:1-4	Genesis 28:13-15	Genesis 48:8-9	Exodus 20:1-3	Leviticus 23:3
Job 42:1-3, 10	Genesis 29:21-25	Exodus 50:19-21	Exodus 25:8-9	Leviticus 26:3-4
Genesis 12:1-3	Genesis 32:24-28	Exodus 2:5-10	Exodus 26:33	Numbers 11:1-2
Genesis 15:4-6	Genesis 33:4-5	Exodus 4:10-12	Exodus 29:38-39	Numbers 13:26-28
Genesis 17:3-8	Gen. 37:23-24, 28	Exodus 6:6-7	Exodus 31:16-17	Numbers 16:47-48
MEMORY VERSE:	MEMORY VERSE:	MEMORY VERSE:	MEMORY VERSE:	MEMORY VERSE:
Hebrews 11:8	I John 3:18	Genesis 50:20	Galatians 5:14	Deuteronomy 31:8

FOUNDATIONS OUTLINE

WEEK 11
OLDER SCRIPTURE
Numbers 20:7-11
Numbers 34:13-15
Deuteronomy 2:2-7
Deuteronomy 4:1-5
Deuteronomy 6:4-9

YOUNGER SCRIPTURE
Numbers 20:10-11
Numbers 34:13
Deuteronomy 2:7
Deuteronomy 4:1-2
Deuteronomy 6:5-6

MEMORY VERSE:
Deuteronomy 4:7

WEEK 12
OLDER SCRIPTURE
Deuteronomy 8:1-6
Dt. 30:11, 19-20
Dt. 34:5, 9-12
Joshua 1:6-9
Joshua 4:1-7

YOUNGER SCRIPTURE
Deuteronomy 8:1-2
Dt. 30:20
Dt. 34:5, 9
Joshua 1:8-9
Joshua 4:4-7

MEMORY VERSE:
Joshua 1:9

WEEK 13
OLDER SCRIPTURE
Joshua 6:2-5
Joshua 7:1, 10-12
Joshua 23:6-10
Judges 3:7-11
Judges 4:1-5

YOUNGER SCRIPTURE
Joshua 6:3-5
Joshua 7:1
Joshua 23:6-8
Judges 3:7-8
Judges 4:4-5

MEMORY VERSE:
Joshua 24:14

WEEK 14
OLDER SCRIPTURE
Judges 6:19-23
Judges 13:24-25
Judges 16:18-20
Ruth 1:15-18, 22
Ruth 4:9-12

YOUNGER SCRIPTURE
Judges 6:19-21
Judges 13:24-25
Judges 16:19-20
Ruth 1:15-16, 22
Ruth 4:9-10

MEMORY VERSE:
Psalm 19:14

WEEK 15
OLDER SCRIPTURE
1 Samuel 1:21-28
1 Samuel 3:7-10
1 Samuel 10:17-24
1 Samuel 13:13-14
1 Sam. 16:5-7, 11-13

YOUNGER SCRIPTURE
1 Samuel 1:26-28
1 Samuel 3:10
1 Samuel 10:17-19
1 Samuel 13:14
1 Samuel 16:11-13

MEMORY VERSE:
1 Samuel 16:7

WEEK 16
OLDER SCRIPTURE
1 Sam. 17:48-51
1 Samuel 19:1-3
1 Samuel 22:1-2
Psalm 22:27-28
1 Sam. 28:15-19

YOUNGER SCRIPTURE
1 Sam. 17:48-50
1 Samuel 19:1-2
1 Samuel 22:1-2
Psalm 22:27-28
1 Sam. 28:15-17

MEMORY VERSE:
2 Timothy 4:17a

WEEK 17
OLDER SCRIPTURE
2 Samuel 2:5-7
Psalm 23
2 Samuel 7:8-11
2 Samuel 9:3-7
2 Samuel 12:7-10

YOUNGER SCRIPTURE
2 Samuel 2:5-7
Psalm 23:1-3
2 Samuel 7:8-9
2 Samuel 9:6-7
2 Samuel 12:7-9

MEMORY VERSE:
Psalm 51:10

WEEK 18
OLDER SCRIPTURE
Psalm 51:1-5
Psalm 24:7-10
Psalm 1:1-3
Psalm 119:9-11
Ps. 119:105-108

YOUNGER SCRIPTURE
Psalm 51:2-4
Psalm 24:7-10
Psalm 1:1-2
Psalm 119:9-11
Ps. 119:105-106

MEMORY VERSE:
Psalm 119:11

WEEK 19
OLDER SCRIPTURE
Psalm 139:1-3
Psalm 150
1 Kings 2:1-4
1 Kings 3:7-12
1 Kings 8:56-61

YOUNGER SCRIPTURE
Psalm 139:1-3
Psalm 150
1 Kings 2:1-3
1 Kings 7:9-12
1 Kings 8:59-61

MEMORY VERSE:
Psalm 139:1-2

WEEK 20
OLDER SCRIPTURE
Proverbs 1:1-7
Proverbs 3:1-6
Pr. 16: 2, 18-19
Proverbs 31:8-9
1 Kings 11:9-11

YOUNGER SCRIPTURE
Proverbs 1:7
Proverbs 3:5-6
Proverbs 16: 2, 18
Proverbs 31:8-9
1 Kings 11:9-10

MEMORY VERSE:
Proverbs 1:7

WEEK 21
OLDER SCRIPTURE
1 Kings 17:1-7
1 Kings 18:36-39
1 Kings 21:25-29
2 Kings 2:11-12
2 Kings 5:9-14

YOUNGER SCRIPTURE
1 Kings 17:1-7
1 Kings 18:36-39
1 Kings 21:25-29
2 Kings 2:11-12
2 Kings 5:14

MEMORY VERSE:
Psalm 63:1

WEEK 22
OLDER SCRIPTURE
Jon. 1:1-4, 15-17; 2:10
Jonah 3:1-5, 10
Hosea 3:4-5
Amos 1:1; 9:7-10
Joel 1:1-4

YOUNGER SCRIPTURE
Jon. 1:1-4, 15-17; 2:10
Jonah 3:4-5, 10
Hosea 3:4-5
Amos 1:1; 9:8
Joel 1:2-3

MEMORY VERSE:
John 11:25

WEEK 23
OLDER SCRIPTURE
Isaiah 9:6-7
Isaiah 44:24-26
Isaiah 53:6
Isaiah 65:17-19
Micah 4:6-7

YOUNGER SCRIPTURE
Isaiah 9:6
Isaiah 44:24-26
Isaiah 53:6
Isaiah 65:17-19
Micah 4:6-7

MEMORY VERSE:
Isaiah 53:6

WEEK 24
OLDER SCRIPTURE
2 Kings 17:6-11
2 Kings 19:15-19
2 Kings 23:1-3
Jeremiah 1:4-8
Jeremiah 29:10-14

YOUNGER SCRIPTURE
2 Kings 17:6-7
2 Kings 19:15-19
2 Kings 23:1-3
Jeremiah 1:4-5
Jeremiah 29:10-14

MEMORY VERSE:
Proverbs 29:18

WEEK 25
OLDER SCRIPTURE
Jeremiah 31:31-34
2 Kings 25:8-12
Ezekiel 37:20-24
Daniel 2:27-30
Daniel 3:24-28

YOUNGER SCRIPTURE
Jeremiah 31:31
2 Kings 25:8-9
Ezekiel 37:21-22
Daniel 2:28-29
Daniel 3:24-28

MEMORY VERSE:
Ezekiel 36:26

WEEK 26

OLDER SCRIPTURE

Daniel 6:19-22
Daniel 12:8-10
Ezra 1:1-4
Ezra 3:10-13
Ezra 6:16-18

YOUNGER SCRIPTURE

Daniel 6:19-22
Daniel 12:8-10
Ezra 1:1-4
Ezra 3:10-11
Ezra 6:16

MEMORY VERSE:

Daniel 9:19

WEEK 27

OLDER SCRIPTURE

Zechariah 1:1-6
Ezra 7:8-10
Ezra 10:1-2
Esther 2:15-18
Esther 4:13-17

YOUNGER SCRIPTURE

Zechariah 1:3
Ezra 7:10
Ezra 10:1-2
Esther 2:17
Esther 4:13-14

MEMORY VERSE:

1 Peter 3:15

WEEK 28

OLDER SCRIPTURE

Esther 7:1-6
Esther 9:20-22
Nehemiah 2:1-6
Neh. 4:7-8, 15-17
Neh. 6:15-16

YOUNGER SCRIPTURE

Esther 7:3-6
Esther 9:20-22
Nehemiah 2:4-6
Neh. 4:7-8, 16-17
Neh. 6:15-16

MEMORY VERSE:

Dt. 29:29

WEEK 29

OLDER SCRIPTURE

Nehemiah 8:2-6
Nehemiah 9:1-3
Neh. 10:28-29
Nehemiah 11:1-2
Neh. 12:27-30

YOUNGER SCRIPTURE

Nehemiah 8:5-6
Nehemiah 9:1-3
Neh. 10:28-29
Nehemiah 11:1-2
Neh. 12:27-30

MEMORY VERSE:

Nehemiah 9:6

WEEK 30

OLDER SCRIPTURE

Neh. 13:17-18
Malachi 1:6-8
Malachi 2:10
Malachi 3:7-12
Malachi 4:4-6

YOUNGER SCRIPTURE

Neh. 13:17-18
Malachi 1:6
Malachi 2:10
Malachi 3:10-12
Malachi 4:4-6

MEMORY VERSE:

Psalm 51:17

WEEK 31

OLDER SCRIPTURE

Luke 1:13-17
Luke 2:4-7, 11-12
Mt. 2:1-2, 9-12
Mark 1:9-11
John 1:1-5, 14

YOUNGER SCRIPTURE

Luke 1:13-14
Luke 2:4-7, 11-12
Mt. 2:1-2, 9-12
Mark 1:9-11
John 1:1-2, 14

MEMORY VERSE:

John 1:1-2

WEEK 32

OLDER SCRIPTURE

Mt. 4:1, 10-11
Matthew 5:43-48
Matthew 6:9-15
Matthew 7:13-14
Matthew 8:14-17

YOUNGER SCRIPTURE

Mt. 4:1, 10-11
Matthew 5:43-48
Matthew 6:9-15
Matthew 7:13-14
Matthew 8:14-17

MEMORY VERSE:

Matthew 6:33

WEEK 33

OLDER SCRIPTURE

Luke 9:46-48
Mark 9:23-24
Luke 12:31-34
John 4:13-15
Luke 14:12-14

YOUNGER SCRIPTURE

Luke 9:46-48
Mark 9:23-24
Luke 12:31-34
John 4:13-15
Luke 14:12-14

MEMORY VERSE:

Luke 14:27

WEEK 34

OLDER SCRIPTURE

John 6:35
Mt. 19:23-26
Luke 15:3-7
Luke 18:35-43
Mark 10:13-16

YOUNGER SCRIPTURE

John 6:35
Mt. 19:25-26
Luke 15:3-7
Luke 18:40-43
Mark 10:13-16

MEMORY VERSE:

Mark 10:45

WEEK 35

OLDER SCRIPTURE

John 11: 17, 39-44
John 13:34-35
John 14:5-6
John 16:33
Mt. 24:30-31

YOUNGER SCRIPTURE

John 11:43-44
John 13:34-35
John 14:5-6
John 16:33
Mt. 24:30-31

MEMORY VERSE:

John 13:35

WEEK 36

OLDER SCRIPTURE

Mt. 24:45-47
John 17:1-5
Mt. 27:27-31
Luke 23:44-46
John 19:38-42

YOUNGER SCRIPTURE

Mt. 24:45-47
John 17:1-5
Mt. 27:27-31
Luke 23:44-46
John 19:41-42

MEMORY VERSE:

John 17:3

WEEK 37

OLDER SCRIPTURE

Mark 16:1-8
Luke 24:15-16, 30-35
John 20:24-29
Mt. 28:18-20
Acts 1:6-11

YOUNGER SCRIPTURE

Mark 16:4-7
Luke 24:15-16, 31-32
John 20:24-29
Mt. 28:18-20
Acts 1:8

MEMORY VERSE:

Acts 1:8

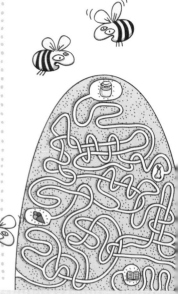

269

WEEK 38
OLDER SCRIPTURE
Acts 2:32-39
Acts 5:12-16
Acts 6:1-6
Acts 7:54-60
Acts 9:1-9

YOUNGER SCRIPTURE
Acts 2:36
Acts 5:12-16
Acts 6:1-6
Acts 7:54-60
Acts 9:3-6

MEMORY VERSE:
Acts 2:42

WEEK 39
OLDER SCRIPTURE
Acts 10:34-36
Acts 12:6-11
Acts 13:1-3
James 2:14-17
James 3:13-18

YOUNGER SCRIPTURE
Acts 10:34-36
Acts 12:6-11
Acts 13:1-3
James 2:14-17
James 3:13

MEMORY VERSE:
James 2:17

WEEK 40
OLDER SCRIPTURE
Acts 16:25-34
Galatians 3:27-29
Galatians 5:13-14
Acts 18:9-11
1 Thess. 1:2-6

YOUNGER SCRIPTURE
Acts 16:29-31
Galatians 3:27-29
Galatians 5:13-14
Acts 18:9-11
1 Thess. 1:2-4

MEMORY VERSE:
Acts 17:24

WEEK 41
OLDER SCRIPTURE
1 Thess. 4:1-2, 7-8
2 Thess. 3:3-5, 13
Acts 19:1-5
1 Cor. 1:26-31
1 Cor. 4:1-5

YOUNGER SCRIPTURE
1 Thess. 4:1-2
2 Thess. 3:13
Acts 19:1-5
1 Cor. 1:30-31
1 Cor. 4:1-2

MEMORY VERSE:
1 Cor. 1:18

WEEK 42
OLDER SCRIPTURE
1 Cor. 6:19-20
1 Cor. 7:23-24
1 Cor. 9:24-27
1 Cor. 12:12-20
1 Cor. 13:4-7

YOUNGER SCRIPTURE
1 Cor. 6:19-20
1 Cor. 7:23-24
1 Cor. 9:24-27
1 Cor. 12:12
1 Cor. 13:4-5

MEMORY VERSE:
1 Cor. 13:13

WEEK 43
OLDER SCRIPTURE
1 Cor. 15:58
2 Cor. 1:20-22
2 Cor. 4:7-10
2 Cor. 5:17-20
2 Cor. 8:1-7

YOUNGER SCRIPTURE
1 Cor. 15:58
2 Cor. 1:20
2 Cor. 4:7-10
2 Cor. 5:17
2 Cor. 8:7

MEMORY VERSE:
Romans 1:16

WEEK 44
OLDER SCRIPTURE
2 Cor. 9:6-8
2 Cor. 12:9-10
Romans 1:16-17
Romans 3:21-24
Romans 5:6-8

YOUNGER SCRIPTURE
2 Cor. 9:7
2 Cor. 12:9-10
Romans 1:16-17
Romans 3:23
Romans 5:6-8

MEMORY VERSE:
Romans 5:1

WEEK 45
OLDER SCRIPTURE
Romans 8:28
Romans 10:9-13
Romans 12:1-2
Romans 14:10-12
Romans 15:5-6

YOUNGER SCRIPTURE
Romans 8:28
Romans 10:13
Romans 12:1-2
Romans 14:10-12
Romans 15:5-6

MEMORY VERSE:
Romans 12:2

WEEK 46
OLDER SCRIPTURE
Acts 20:7-12
Acts 23:11
Acts 24:14-16
Acts 27:20-26
Acts 28:23-24

YOUNGER SCRIPTURE
Acts 20:9-10, 12
Acts 23:11
Acts 24:14-16
Acts 27:23-24
Acts 28:23-24

MEMORY VERSE:
2 Corinthians 4:7

WEEK 47
OLDER SCRIPTURE
Colossians 2:6-7
Colossians 3:12-17
Ephesians 2:8-10
Ephesians 4:25-32
Ephesians 6:1-4

YOUNGER SCRIPTURE
Colossians 2:6-7
Colossians 3:12-13
Ephesians 2:8-10
Ephesians 4:25-26
Ephesians 6:1-4

MEMORY VERSE:
Ephesians 2:8-9

WEEK 48
OLDER SCRIPTURE
Philippians 1:20
Philippians 4:11-13
Hebrews 2:18
Hebrews 4:12-13
Hebrews 6:10-12

YOUNGER SCRIPTURE
Philippians 1:20
Philippians 4:13
Hebrews 2:18
Hebrews 4:12-13
Hebrews 6:10-12

MEMORY VERSE:
Philippians 3:7

WEEK 49
OLDER SCRIPTURE
Hebrews 7:24-25
Hebrews 9:11-12
Hebrews 10:23-25
Hebrews 11:1-3
Hebrews 12:1-2

YOUNGER SCRIPTURE
Hebrews 7:24-25
Hebrews 9:11-12
Hebrews 10:23-25
Hebrews 11:1-3
Hebrews 12:1-2

MEMORY VERSE:
2 Corinthians 5:17

WEEK 50
OLDER SCRIPTURE
1 Timothy 3:1-4
1 Timothy 4:11-12
2 Timothy 2:15
2 Timothy 3:13-17
1 Peter 1:13-16

YOUNGER SCRIPTURE
1 Timothy 3:1-4
1 Timothy 4:12
2 Timothy 2:15
2 Timothy 3:16-17
1 Peter 1:13-16

MEMORY VERSE:
2 Timothy 2:15

WEEK 51
OLDER SCRIPTURE
1 Peter 4:8-11
1 Peter 5:5-7
2 Peter 3:17-18
1 John 1:5-9
1 John 4:7-12

YOUNGER SCRIPTURE
1 Peter 4:8-11
1 Peter 5:5-7
2 Peter 3:17-18
1 John 1:9
1 John 4:11

MEMORY VERSE:
1 John 4:11

WEEK 52
OLDER SCRIPTURE
Revelation 1:17-19
Revelation 2:7
Revelation 4:11
Revelation 19:11-13
Revelation 21:5-7

YOUNGER SCRIPTURE
Revelation 1:17-19
Revelation 2:7
Revelation 4:11
Revelation 19:11-13
Revelation 21:5-7

MEMORY VERSE:
Revelation 3:19

Disciple-Making Resources

Replicate.org

Our Replicate website is packed with tools to help create awareness for disciple-making. In addition to downloads and web-based content, the Replicate blog is a great source of insight and commentary on the current state of disciple-making.

The Replicate Disciple-Making Podcast

Beginning summer 2016 the Replicate Disciple-Making Podcast will host discussions with key leaders who have a passion for discipleship as well as sharing practical principles to help listeners engage in disciple-making.

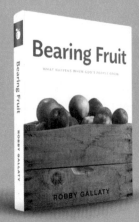

The Growing Up Series

01 Growing Up. *Growing Up* is a practical, easy-to-implement system for growing in one's faith. It is a manual for making disciples, addressing the what, why, where, and how of discipleship. *Growing Up* provides you with transferrable principles for creating and working with discipleship groups, allowing you to gain positive information both for yourself and for others as you learn how to help others become better disciples for Christ.

02 Firmly Planted. Why Is spiritual growth complicated? *Firmly Planted* is the second book in the Growing Up series. In biblical, practical, and simple terms, the book shares a roadmap for spiritual maturity. *Firmly Planted* addresses topics such as how you can be sure of your salvation, why your identity in Christ affects everything you do, how to overcome the three enemies that cripple a Christian's growth, a battle plan for gaining victory over temptation, and the indispensable spiritual discipline every believer must foster.

03 Bearing Fruit. *Bearing Fruit* is the third book in the Growing Up series. In this book, the reader will understand how God grows believers. Robby identifies seven places the word "fruit" is found in the bible: fruit of holiness, fruit of righteousness, fruit of soul-winning, fruit of the spirit, fruit of the praise, fruit of repentance, and fruit of giving. You will understand your role in the fruit bearing process of spiritual growth. *Bearing Fruit* is applicable for new and mature believers alike.